THE MOST EXCELLENT HISTORIE OF

The Merchant of Venice

In the same series

**PRENTICE HALL
HARVESTER WHEATSHEAF**

LONDON • NEW YORK • TORONTO • SYDNEY • TOKYO • SINGAPORE •
MADRID • MEXICO CITY • MUNICH

SHAKESPEAREAN ORIGINALS:
FIRST EDITIONS

———

THE MOST EXCELLENT HISTORIE OF

The Merchant of Venice

EDITED AND INTRODUCED BY
ANNABEL PATTERSON

PRENTICE HALL

HARVESTER WHEATSHEAF

First published 1995 by
Prentice Hall International (UK) Limited
Campus 400, Maylands Avenue
Hemel Hempstead
Hertfordshire HP2 7EZ
A division of
Simon & Schuster International Group

Designed by Geoff Green

Typeset in 11pt Bembo
by Photoprint, Torquay, Devon

Printed and bound in Great Britain by
Biddles Ltd, Guildford and King's Lynn

Library of Congress Cataloging-in-Publication Data

Shakespeare, William, 1564–1616.
 [Merchant of Venice]
 The most excellent historie of The merchant of
Venice / edited and introduced by Annabel Patterson.
  p. cm. — (Shakespearean originals—first editions)
 Includes bibliographical references (p.).
 ISBN 0–13–355520–8
 1. Jews—Italy—Venice—Drama. I. Patterson,
Annabel M. II. Title. III. Series.
PR2750.B25 1995
822.3'3—dc20
                                             95–7564
                                                CIP

British Library Cataloguing in Publication Data

A catalogue record for this book is available from
the British Library
ISBN 0–13–355520–8

1 2 3 4 5   99 98 97 96 95

Contents

General Introduction

THIS series puts into circulation single annotated editions of early modern play-texts whose literary and theatrical histories have been overshadowed by editorial practices dominant since the eighteenth century.

The vast majority of Shakespeare's modern readership encounters his works initially through the standard modernised editions of the major publishing houses, whose texts form the basis of innumerable playhouse productions and classroom discussions. While these textualisations vary considerably in terms of approach and detail, the overwhelming impression they foster is not of diversity but uniformity: the same plays are reprinted in virtually identical words, within a ubiquitous, standardised format. Cumulatively, such texts serve to constitute and define a particular model of Shakespeare's work, conjuring up a body of writing which is given and stable, handed down by the author like holy writ. But the canonical status of these received texts is ultimately dependent not upon a divine creator, but upon those editorial mediations (rendered transparent by the discursive authority of the very texts they ostensibly serve) that shape the manner in which Shakespeare's works are produced and reproduced within contemporary culture.

Many modern readers of Shakespeare, lulled by long-established editorial traditions into an implicit confidence in the object of their attention, probably have little idea of what a sixteenth-century printed play-text actually looked like. Confronted with an example, she or he could be forgiven for recoiling before the intimidating display of linguistic and visual strangeness – antique type, non-standardised spelling, archaic orthographic conventions, unfamiliar and irregular speech prefixes, oddly placed stage directions, and

[1]

possibly an absence of Act and scene divisions. 'It looks more like Chaucer than Shakespeare,' observed one student presented with a facsimile of an Elizabethan text, neatly calling attention to the peculiar elisions through which Shakespeare is accepted as modern, while Chaucer is categorised as ancient. A student reading Chaucer in a modern translation knows that the text is a contemporary version, not a historical document. But the modern translations of Shakespeare which almost universally pass as accurate and authentic representations of an original – the standard editions – offer themselves as simultaneously historical document and accessible modern version – like a tidily restored ancient building.

The earliest versions of Shakespeare's works existed in plural and contested forms. Some nineteen of those plays modern scholars now attribute to Shakespeare (together with the non-dramatic verse) appeared in cheap Quarto format during his life, their theatrical provenance clearly marked by an emphasis upon the companies who owned and produced the plays rather than the author.[1] Where rival Quartos of a play were printed, these could contrast starkly: the Second Quarto of *The tragicall historie of Hamlet, prince of Denmarke* (1604), for example, is almost double the length of its First Quarto (1603) predecessor and renames many of the leading characters. In 1623, Shakespeare's colleagues Heminges and Condell brought out posthumously the prestigious and expensive First Folio, the earliest collected edition of his dramatic works. This included major works, such as *The Tragedy of Macbeth*, *The Tragedie of Antonie, and Cleopater*, and *The Tempest*, which had never before been published. It also contained versions of those plays, with the exception of *Pericles*, which had earlier appeared in quarto versions which in some cases differ so markedly from their notional predecessors for them to be regarded not simply as variants of a single work, but as discrete textualisations independently framed within a complex and diversified project of cultural production; perhaps, even, in some senses, as separate plays. In the case of *Hamlet*, for example, the Folio includes some eighty lines which are not to be found in the Second Quarto, yet omits a fragment of around 230 lines which includes Hamlet's final soliloquy;[2] and far greater differences exist between certain other pairings.

This relatively fluid textual situation continued throughout the seventeenth century. Quartos of individual plays continued to appear sporadically, usually amended reprints of earlier editions, but occasionally introducing new works, such as the first publication of Shakespeare and Fletcher's *The two noble kinsmen* (1634), a play which was perhaps excluded from the Folio on the basis of its collaborative status.[3] The title of another work written in collaboration with Fletcher, *Cardenio*, was entered on the Stationer's Register of 1653, but it appears not to have been published and the play is now lost. The First Folio proved a commercial success and was reprinted in 1632, although again amended in detail. In 1663, a third edition appeared which in its 1664 reprinting assigned to Shakespeare seven plays, never before printed in folio, viz. *Pericles Prince of Tyre; The London prodigall; The history of Thomas Ld Cromwell; Sir John Oldcastle Lord Cobham; The Puritan widow; A Yorkshire tragedy; The tragedy of Locrine.* These attributions, moreover, were accepted uncritically by the 1685 Fourth Folio.

The assumptions underlying seventeenth-century editorial practice, particularly the emphasis that the latest edition corrects and subsumes all earlier editions, are rarely explicitly stated. They are graphically illustrated, though, by the Bodleian Library's decision to sell off as surplus to requirements the copy of the First Folio it had acquired in 1623 as soon as the enlarged 1663 edition came into its possession.[4] Eighteenth-century editors continued to work within this tradition. Rowe set his illustrated critical edition from the 1685 Fourth Folio, introducing further emendations and modernisations. Alexander Pope used Rowe as the basis of his own text, but he 'corrected' this liberally, partly on the basis of variants contained with the twenty-eight Quartos he catalogued but more often relying on his own intuitive judgement, maintaining that he was merely 'restoring' Shakespeare to an original purity which had been lost through 'arbitrary Additions, Expunctions, Transpositions of scenes and lines, Confusions of Characters and Persons, wrong application of Speeches, corruptions of innumerable passages'[5] introduced by actors. Although eighteenth-century editors disagreed fiercely over the principles of their task, all of them concurred in finding corruption at every point of textual transmission (and in Capell's case, composition), and sought the restoration of a perceived poetic genius: for Theobald, Warburton, Johnson and Steevens,

General Introduction

'The multiple sources of corruption justified editorial intervention; in principle at least, the edition that had received the most editorial attention, the most recent edition, was the purest because the most purified.'[6]

This conception of the editorial function was decisively challenged in theory and practice by Edmund Malone, who substituted the principles of archaeology for those of evolution. For Malone, there could be only one role for an editor: to determine what Shakespeare himself had written. Those texts which were closest to Shakespeare in time were therefore the only true authority; the accretions from editorial interference in the years which followed the publication of the First Folio and early quartos had to be stripped away to recover the original. Authenticity, that is, was to be based on restoration understood not as improvement but as rediscovery. The methodology thus offered the possibility that the canon of Shakespeare's works could be established decisively, fixed for all time, by reference to objective, historical criteria. Henceforth, the text of Shakespeare was to be regarded, potentially, as monogenous, derived from a single source, rather than polygenous.

Malone's influence has proved decisive to the history of nineteenth- and twentieth-century bibliographic studies. Despite, however, the enormous growth in knowledge concerning the material processes of Elizabethan and Jacobean book production, the pursuit of Shakespeare's original words sanctioned a paradoxical distrust of precisely those early texts which Malone regarded as the touchstone of authenticity. Many assumed that these texts must themselves have been derived from some kind of authorial manuscript, and the possibility that Shakespeare's papers lay hidden somewhere exercised an insidious fascination upon the antiquarian imagination. Libraries were combed, lofts ransacked, and graves plundered, but the manuscripts have proved obstinately elusive, mute testimony to the low estimate an earlier culture had placed upon them once performance and publication had exhausted their commercial value.

Undeterred, scholars attempted to infer from the evidence of the early printed texts the nature of the manuscript which lay behind them. The fact that the various extant versions differed so considerably from each other posed a problem which could only be partially resolved by the designation of some as 'Bad Quartos', and therefore non-Shakespearean; for even the remaining 'authorised' texts varied between themselves enormously, invariably in terms of detail and often in terms of substance. Recourse to the concept of manuscript authenticity could not resolve the difficulty, for such a manuscript simply does not exist.[7] Faced with apparent textual anarchy, editors sought solace in Platonic idealism: each variant was deemed an imperfect copy of a perfect (if unobtainable) paradigm. Once again, the editor's task was to restore a lost original purity, employing compositor study, collation, conflation and emendation.[8]

Compositor study attempts to identify the working practices of the individuals who set the early Quartos and the Folio, and thus differentiate the non-Shakespearean interference, stripping the 'veil of print from a text' and thus attempting 'to recover a number of precise details of the underlying manuscript'.[9] Collation, the critical comparison of different states of a text with a view to establishing the perfect condition of a particular copy, provided systematic classification of textual variations which could be regarded as putative corruptions. Emendation allows the editor to select one of the variations thrown up by collation and impose it upon the reading of the selected control text, or where no previous reading appeared satisfactory, to introduce a correction based upon editorial judgement. Conflation is employed to resolve the larger scale divergences between texts, so that, for example, the Folio *Tragedie of Hamlet, Prince of Denmarke* is often employed as the control text for modern editions of the play, but since it 'lacks' entire passages found only in the Second Quarto, these are often grafted on to the former to create the fullest 'authoritative' text.

The cuts to the Folio *Hamlet* may reflect, however, not a corruption introduced in the process of transmission, but a deliberate alteration to the text authorised by the dramatist himself. In recent years, the proposition that Shakespeare revised his work and that texts might therefore exist in a variety of forms has attracted considerable support. The most publicised debate has centred on the relationship of the Quarto *M. William Shak-speare: his true chronicle historie of the life and death of King Lear and his three daughters* and the Folio *Tragedie of King Lear*.[10] The editors of the recent Oxford Shakespeare have broken new ground by including both texts in their one-volume edition on the grounds that the *Tragedie* represents an authorial revision of the earlier *Historie*, which is sufficiently radical to justify classifying it as a separate play. Wells and Taylor founded their revisionist position upon a recognition of the fact that Shakespeare was primarily a working *dramatist* rather than literary author and that he addressed his play-texts towards a particular audience of theatrical professionals who were expected to flesh out the bare skeleton of the performance script: 'The written text of any such manuscript thus depended upon an unwritten para-text which always accompanied it: an invisible life-support system of stage directions, which Shakespeare could expect his first audience to supply, or which those first readers would expect Shakespeare himself to supply orally.'[11] They are thus more open than many of their predecessors to the possibility that texts reflect their theatrical provenance and therefore that a plurality of authorised texts may exist, at least for certain of the plays.[12] They remain, however, firmly author centred – the invisible life-support system can ultimately always be traced back to the dramatist himself and the plays remain under his parental authority.[13]

What, however, if it were not Shakespeare but the actor Burbage who suggested, or perhaps insisted on, the cuts to *Hamlet*? Would the Folio version of the play become unShakespearean? How would we react if we *knew* that the Clown spoke 'More than is set down' and that his ad libs were recorded? Or that the King's Men sanctioned additions by another dramatist for a Court performance? Or that a particular text recorded not the literary script of a play but its performance script? Of course, in one sense we cannot know these things. But drama, by its very nature, is overdetermined, the product of multiple influences simultaneously operating across a single site of cultural production. Eyewitness accounts of perform-ances of the period suggest something of the provisionality of the scripts Shakespeare provided to his theatrical colleagues:

> After dinner on the 21st of september, at about two o'clock, I went with my companions over the water, and in the thatched playhouse saw the tragedy of the first Emperor Julius with at least fifteen characters very well acted. At the end of the comedy they danced according to their custom with extreme elegance. Two in men's clothes and two in women's gave this performance, in wonderful combination with each other.[14]

This passage offers what can seem a bizarre range of codes; the thatched playhouse, well-acted tragedy, comic aftermath and elegant transvestite dance, hardly correspond to the typology of Shakespearean drama our own culture has appropriated. The Swiss tourist Thomas Platter was in fact fortunate to catch the curious custom of the jig between Caesar and the boy dressed as Caesar's wife, for by 1612 'all Jigs, Rhymes and Dances' after plays had been 'utterly abolished' to prevent 'tumults and outrages whereby His Majesty's Peace is often broke'.[15] Shakespeare, however, is the 'author' of the spectacle Platter witnessed only in an extremely limited sense; in this context the dramatist's surname functions not simply to authenticate a literary masterpiece, but serves as a convenient if misleading shorthand term alluding to the complex material practices of the Elizabethan and Jacobean theatre industry.[16] It is in the latter sense that the term is used in this series.

Modern theoretical perspectives have destabilised the notion of the author as transcendent subject operating outside history and culture. This concept is in any event peculiarly inappropriate when applied to popular drama of the period. It is quite possible that, as Terence Hawkes argues, 'The notion of a single "authoritative" text, immediately expressive of the plenitude of its author's mind and meaning, would have been unfamiliar to Shakespeare, involved as he was in the collaborative enterprise of dramatic production and notoriously unconcerned to preserve in stable form the texts of most of his plays.'[17] The script is, of course, an integral element of drama, but it is by no means the only one. This is obvious in forms of representation, such as film, dependent on technologies which emphasise the role of the *auteur* at the expense of that of the writer. But even in the early modern theatre, dramatic realisation depended not just upon the scriptwriter,[18] but upon actors, entrepreneurs, promptbook keepers, audiences, patrons, etc.; in fact, the entire wide range of professional and institutional interests constituting the theatre industry of the period.

Just as the scriptwriter cannot be privileged over all other influences, nor can any single script. It is becoming clear that within Elizabethan and Jacobean culture, around each 'Shakespeare' play there circulated a wide variety of texts, performing different theatrical functions and adopting different shapes in different contexts of production. Any of these contexts may be of interest to the modern reader. The so-called Bad Quartos, for example, are generally marginalised as piratically published versions based upon the memorial reconstructions of the plays by bit-part actors. But even if the theory of memorial reconstruction is correct (and it is considerably more controversial than is generally recognised[19]), these Quarto texts would provide a unique window on to the plays as they were originally performed and open up exciting opportunities for contemporary performance.[20] They form part, that is, of a rich diversity of textual variation which is shrouded by those traditional editorial practices which have sought to impose a single, 'ideal' paradigm.

In this series we have sought to build upon the pioneering work of Wells and Taylor, albeit along quite different lines. They argue, for example, that

> The lost manuscripts of Shakespeare's work are not the fiction of an idealist critic, but particular material objects which happen at a particular time to have existed, and at another particular time to have been lost, or to have ceased to exist. Emendation does not seek to construct an ideal text, but rather to restore certain features of a lost material object (that manuscript) by correcting certain apparent deficiencies in a second material object (this printed text) which purports to be a copy of the first. Most readers will find this procedure reasonable enough.[21]

The important emphasis here is on the relative status of the two forms, manuscript and printed text: the object of which we can have direct knowledge, the printed text, is judged to be corrupt by conjectural reference to the object of which we can by definition have no direct knowledge, the uncorrupted (but non-existent) manuscript. This corresponds to no philosophical materialism we have encountered. The editors of *Shakespearean Originals* reject the claim that it is possible to construct a rehabilitated text reflecting a form approximating Shakespeare's artistic vision.[22] Instead we prefer to embrace the early printed texts as authentic material objects, the concrete forms from which all subsequent editions ultimately derive.

We therefore present within this series particular textualisations of plays which are not necessarily canonical or indeed even written by *William Shakespeare, Gent*, in the traditional sense; but which nevertheless represent important facets of Shakespearean drama. In the same way that we have rejected the underlying principles of traditional editorial practice, we have also approached traditional editorial procedures with extreme caution, preferring to let the texts speak for themselves with a minimum of editorial mediation. We refuse to allow speculative judgements concerning the exact contribution of the various individuals involved in the production of a given text the authority to license alterations to that text, and as a result relegate compositor study and collation[23] to the textual apparatus rather than attempt to incorporate them into the text itself through emendation.

It seems to us that there is in fact no philosophical justification for emendation, which foregrounds the editor at the expense of the text. The distortions introduced by this process are all too readily incorporated into the text as holy writ. Macbeth's famous lines, for example, 'I dare do all that may become a man, / Who dares do more, is none,' on closer inspection turn out to be Rowe's. The Folio reads, 'I dare do all that may become a man, / Who dares no more is none.' There seems to us no pressing reason whatsoever to alter these lines,[24] and we prefer to confine all such editorial speculation to the critical apparatus. The worst form of emendation is conflation. It is now widely recognised that the texts of *M. William Shak-speare: his true chronicle historie of King Lear and his three daughters* (1608) and *The Tragedie of King Lear* (1623) differ so markedly that they must be considered as two distinct plays and that the composite *King Lear* which is reproduced in every twentieth-century popular edition of the play is a hybrid which grossly distorts both the originals from which it is derived. We believe that the case of *Lear* is a particularly clear example of a general proposition: that *whenever* distinct textualisations are conflated, the result is a hybrid without independent value. It should therefore go without saying that all the texts in this series are based upon single sources.

The most difficult editorial decisions we have had to face concern the modernisation of these texts. In some senses we have embarked upon a project of textual archaeology and the logic of our position points towards facsimile editions. These, however, are already available in specialist libraries, where they are there marginalised by

General Introduction

those processes of cultural change which have rendered them alien and forbidding. Since we wish to challenge the hegemony of standard editions by circulating the texts within this series as widely as possible, we have aimed at 'diplomatic' rather than facsimile status and have modernised those orthographic and printing conventions (such as long s, positional variants of u and v, i and j, ligatures and contractions) which are no longer current and likely to confuse. We do so, however, with some misgiving, recognising that as a result certain possibilities open to the Elizabethan reader are thereby foreclosed. On the other hand, we make no attempt to standardise such features as speech prefixes and *dramatis personae*, or impose conventions derived from naturalism, such as scene divisions and locations, upon the essentially fluid and non-naturalistic medium of the Elizabethan theatre. In order that our own editorial practice should be as open as possible we provide as an appendix a sample of the original text in photographic facsimile.

GRAHAM HOLDERNESS AND BRYAN LOUGHREY

NOTES AND REFERENCES

1. The title page of the popular *Titus Andronicus*, for example, merely records that it was 'Plaide by the Right Honourable the Earle of Darbie, Earle of Pembrooke, and Earle of Sussex their Servants', and not until 1598 was Shakespeare's name attached to a printed version of one of his plays, *Love's Labour's Lost*.
2. For a stimulating discussion of the relationship between the three texts of *Hamlet*, see Steven Urkowitz, '"Well-sayd olde Mole", Burying Three *Hamlets* in Modern Editions', in Georgianna Ziegler (ed.), *Shakespeare Study Today* (New York: AMS Press, 1986), pp. 37–70.
3. In the year of Shakespeare's death Ben Jonson staked a far higher claim for the status of the playwright, bringing out the first ever collected edition of English dramatic texts, *The Workes of Beniamin Jonson*, a carefully prepared and expensively produced folio volume. The text of his Roman tragedy *Sejanus*, a play originally written with an unknown collaborator, was carefully revised to preserve the purity of authorial input. See Bryan Loughrey and Graham Holderness, 'Shakespearean Features', in Jean Marsden (ed.), *The Appropriation of Shakespeare: Post-Renaissance Reconstructions of the Works and the Myth* (Hemel Hempstead: Harvester Wheatsheaf, 1991), p. 183.

General Introduction

4. F. Madan and G.M.R. Turbutt (eds), *The Original Bodleian Copy of the First Folio of Shakespeare* (Oxford: Oxford University Press, 1905), p. 5.
5. Cited in D. Nicol Smith, *Eighteenth Century Essays* (Oxford: Oxford University Press, 1963), p. 48.
6. Margreta de Grazia, *Shakespeare Verbatim* (Oxford: Oxford University Press, 1991), p. 62. De Grazia provides the fullest and most stimulating account of the important theoretical issues raised by eighteenth-century editorial practice.
7. Unless the Hand D fragment of 'The Booke of Sir Thomas Moore' (British Library Harleian MS 7368) really is that of Shakespeare. See Stanley Wells and Gary Taylor, *William Shakespeare: A Textual Companion* (Oxford: Oxford University Press, 1987), pp. 461–7.
8. See Margreta de Grazia, 'The Essential Shakespeare and the Material Book', *Textual Practice*, vol. 2, no. 1 (Spring 1988).
9. Fredson Bowers, 'Textual Criticism', in O.J. Campbell and E.G. Quinn (eds), *The Reader's Encyclopedia of Shakespeare* (New York: Methuen, 1966), p. 869.
10. See, for example, Gary Taylor and Michael Warren (eds), *The Division of the Kingdoms* (Oxford: Oxford University Press, 1983).
11. Stanley Wells and Gary Taylor, *William Shakespeare: A Textual Companion* (Oxford: Oxford University Press, 1987), p. 2.
12. See, for example, Stanley Wells, 'Plural Shakespeare', *Critical Survey*, vol. 1, no. 1 (Spring 1989).
13. See, for example, *Textual Companion*, p. 69.
14. Thomas Platter, a Swiss physician who visited London in 1599 and recorded his playgoing; cited in *The Reader's Encyclopaedia*, p. 634. For a discussion of this passage see Richard Wilson, *Julius Caesar: A Critical Study* (Harmondsworth: Penguin, 1992), chapter 3.
15. E.K. Chambers, *The Elizabethan Stage* (Oxford: Oxford University Press, 1923), pp. 340–1.
16. The texts of the plays sometimes encode the kind of stage business Platter recorded. The epilogue of *2 Henry IV*, for example, is spoken by a dancer who announces that 'My tongue is weary; when my legs are too, I will bid you good night . . .'
17. Terence Hawkes, *That Shakespeherian Rag* (London, Methuen, 1986), p. 75.
18. For a discussion of Shakespeare's texts as dramatic scripts, see Jonathan Bate, 'Shakespeare's Tragedies as Working Scripts', *Critical Survey*, vol. 3, no. 2 (1991), pp. 118–27.
19. See, for example, Random Cloud [Randall McLeod], 'The Marriage of

[11]

General Introduction

Good and Bad Quartos', *Shakespeare Quarterly*, vol. 33, no. 4 (1982), pp. 421–30.

20. See, for example, Bryan Loughrey, 'Q1 in Modern Performance', in Tom Clayton (ed.), *The 'Hamlet' First Published* (Newark, University of Delaware Press, 1992) and Nicholas Shrimpton, 'Shakespeare Performances in London and Stratford-Upon-Avon, 1984–5', *Shakespeare Survey* 39, pp. 193–7.

21. *Textual Companion*, p. 60.

22. The concept of authorial intention, which has generated so much debate amongst critics, remains curiously unexamined within the field of textual studies.

23. Charlton Hinman's Norton Facsimile of *The First Folio of Shakespeare* offers a striking illustration of why this should be so. Hinman set out to reproduce the text of the original First Folio, but his collation of the Folger Library's numerous copies demonstrated that 'every copy of the finished book shows a mixture of early and late states of the text that is peculiar to it alone'. He therefore selected from the various editions those pages he believed represented the printer's final intentions and bound these together to produce something which 'has hitherto been only a theoretical entity, an abstraction: *the* First Folio'. Thus the technology which would have allowed him to produce a literal facsimile in fact is deployed to create an ahistorical composite which differs in substance from every single original upon which it is based. See Charlton Hinman, *The First Folio of Shakespeare* (New York, 1968), pp. xxiii–xxiv.

24. Once the process begins, it becomes impossible to adjudicate between rival conjectural emendations. In this case, for example, Hunter's suggestion that Lady Macbeth should be given the second of these lines seems to us neither more nor less persuasive than Rowe's.

Introduction

T H E Quarto version of *The Most excellent Historie of the Merchant of Venice* has exceptionally good credentials among early Shakespearean printed texts, as John Russell Brown, for the Arden edition, M.M. Mahood, for the New Cambridge edition, and Jay Halio, for the World's Classics, have testified; and the case for its appearance in the *Shakespearean Originals* series can therefore be made rather differently from that required by, for example, *The Cronicle History of Henry the fift* or the 1603 Quarto of *Hamlet*. The 1600 Quarto has long been recognised as an unusually clean and intelligent text, almost free from obvious errors, and, more importantly, showing signs of having been printed either directly from Shakespeare's own manuscript or, less likely as the fashion for positing intermediary versions recedes, a fair copy thereof. The First Folio of 1623 included a version of the play that was itself based on the 1600 Quarto, with only a few small changes, some of them introduced to bring the dialogue into line with Jacobean restrictions on profanity or other sensitivities. This makes the 1600 Quarto a 'Shakespearean Original' in two senses simultaneously, being both the version of the play that Elizabethan audiences at the turn of the century bought and read (and almost certainly saw, since no traces exist of other versions), and the one that records indisputably Shakespeare's intentions – at least so far as what words should be spoken on the stage. Unlike the instances of *The Cronicle History* or the First Quarto of *Hamlet*, which are so different from the versions traditionally considered authoritative that there are grounds for seeing them as separate or alternative plays, *The Most excellent Historie of the Merchant of Venice* has sufficient philosophical self-identity to satisfy the idealist – the believer in definitive texts which

Introduction

can fully represent autonomous acts of creation – along with some very interesting signs of historical contingency and fossilised evidence of the materiality of printing.

This is not to claim that a diplomatic text of the play is *better* than modern editions, to which I am inevitably indebted, especially the three already mentioned, which have brought the art of compromise to a state of extraordinary polish. Nevertheless, when presented without tidying and shaping (division into acts and scenes, normalisation of speech prefixes, relineations, emendations, not to mention modernised spelling), the 1600 Quarto offers its readers a unique experience: more or less direct contact with Shakespeare as writer and thinker, writing fast and smoothly in seemingly effortless verse. The few mistakes produced by the compositors, and the way they dealt with the exigencies of typesetting, rather clarify than obscure some features of the play that we might otherwise miss. We can observe Shakespeare making a few mistakes of his own in the naming of characters and places; but we can also detect some of his habits, of orthography, punctuation, and even of thought. And from the special effects in the casket scenes to the rapid and symbolic interchange of the Venice/Belmont plots, more visible here than when sliced and spaced by modern typography, the Quarto gives the reader an intensely *lively* experience of the play's insistence on repetition, balance and ritual action.

These formulaic aspects of the play are essential to its ultimate finessing of the intellectual and moral problems it raises, and the central device by which the disturbing forces unleashed by Shylock are formally contained. The otherwise shabby and untrustworthy promise of a 'happy ending' can therefore seem fulfilled, at least in the theatre; but in a text for reading – and that *The Most excellent Historie of the Merchant of Venice* appeared in four quarto editions over more than half a century implies considerable readerly interest – details of the play's texture become most uncomically worrisome.

To begin with, what the 1600 Quarto insists on our noticing, and a modern edition obscures, is the bias, indeed the misinformation by which bias was intensified, designed to attract the late Elizabethan reader. The title page withheld the information that the play was a comedy; instead, the potential buyer was lured in by reference to

[14]

'the extreame crueltie of *Shylocke* the Jewe towards the sayd Merchant', not in planning an attempt on his life, but in actually '*cutting* a just pound of his flesh'.[1] The significance of this in the later Quarto tradition will be discussed below; but here it is enough to note that the 'Historie' so advertised exerted strong ideological controls over reader expectations, controls which were subsequently discovered to be untrustworthy. How far this mistrust might extend in the seventeenth century, and what else might support it, is a problem incapable of determination; but the 1600 Quarto and its printing history give *some* evidence that anti-Semitism as a cultural assumption was more productive of anxiety in early modern England than is likely to be granted by today's Shakespeareans of whatever creed or camp.

The evidence that the 1600 Quarto was printed from Shakespeare's holograph is both complex and contested. It shares certain features with the Second Quarto of *Hamlet*, also thought to be set from holograph, and the Hand D additions to *Sir Thomas More*, which are now generally taken to be in Shakespeare's handwriting. These include a decrease, amounting to virtually a disappearance, of capital letters at the beginning of verse lines; a light use of punctuation, with a preference for commas where we would use a heavier form of stop; and certain spellings – 'farwell', 'sayd', 'howre', and, more striking, 'a leven' instead of 'eleven'. To assume that in producing these features the compositor was *reproducing* Shakespeare's practice, we must combine certain kinds of logic (a playwright, writing fast, would not naturally capitalise at the beginning of lines), with the researches of scholars into the habits of compositors. John Russell Brown has shown that the compositors who set the 1600 Quarto were 'careful and conservative' in reproducing the spelling and punctuation of their copy, and that their light punctuation in this instance is not typical of their work.[2]

Because both *Hamlet* Q2 and the 1600 Quarto were set by the same compositors, and because, whereas the latter is a very fine text, the Second Quarto *Hamlet* is full of errors and confusions, it has been argued they cannot both be from holograph.[3] But M.M. Mahood's response is that logically they can, since authorial manuscripts may themselves be clean or confusing to read, depending on the stage in the compositional process they record. 'Too much has been made,' she argues, 'of the discrepancy with *Hamlet*; the legibility of the Hand D additions should shift the problem from "Why is *The Merchant of Venice* Q1 such a good text?" to "Why is the text of *Hamlet* Q2 so bad?".'[4] In addition, the very fact that we have three versions of *Hamlet*, and that Shakespeareans still cannot account for all the discrepancies between them, suggests changes of, or struggles within, authorial intention; but from the opening lines, *The Most excellent Historie of the Merchant of Venice*, a far less convoluted and convulsed play in every respect but one, unrolls like an oriental carpet, its design and diction calm and predictable.

The features of the 1600 Quarto that suggest an authorial manuscript include a variety of small mistakes in naming and signifying entrances, the presence of certain stage directions that are atypical of prompt books, and the absence of some that would be typical. Stage directions like 'Enter *Portia* with her wayting woman *Nerrissa*', '*Enter* Bassanio *with a follower or two*', 'Enter *Morochus* a tawnie Moore all in white, and three or four followers accordingly', *Enter Jewe and his man that was the Clowne*', and '*A Song the whilst Bassanio comments on the caskets to himselfe*' are unlikely to derive from a prompt book, since they contain more narrative explanation than needed in the theatre, while the vagueness about numbers in 'a follower or two' or 'three or four followers' would have disappeared with casting. There is a double entry for Tubal, and a missing entry for Portia, of which the second could have been a printer's error, but the first more likely the result of incomplete authorial revision. On the other hand, the Folio provides seven directions for musical effects which do not appear in the Quartos, for example, 'Flor. Cornets', to usher out Morocho and usher in Arragon in their respective trials of the caskets, and 'Here music', to cue in the song 'Tell me where is fancy bred' which is sung while Bassanio meditates on his choice. When the Folio was set from the 1600 Quarto, these additions must have found their way into it from the more musical Jacobean theatrical tradition.

Other mistakes have the same flavour; that is, of the authorial draft. Portia sends her servant Balthazar to Mantua to set up the arrangements with her cousin Bellario for the trial, but later the Duke knows that Bellario lives in Padua, and Nerrissa agrees. Just to add to the confusion, the pseudonym that Portia adopts as the young Doctor of Law is Balthazar. The puzzle familiarly known as 'the three Sallies' results from variations in the spelling of Salarino and Salanio and their speech-prefixes, which fluctuate so wildly that editors cannot be sure whether the Salerio who appears as a messenger from Venice to bring Bassanio news of Anthonio's financial crisis is one of the two we have met already or a third distinct character. Fortunately, this is a problem whose solution the editor of a diplomatic text may cheerfully leave to others. The alternations between 'Clowne' and 'Launcelet' in the speech prefixes, and between 'Shylocke' and 'Jewe' in both stage directions and speech prefixes, may also suggest a manuscript in rapid composition rather than fair copy; but this also raises the issue of typification as denigration, to which we must return. By similar token, Portia and Nerrissa include six suitors in their xenophobic mocking scene, but the servant who comes to announce the suitors' departure mentions only four. This has caused some editors and producers to imagine that the Scotsman and the Englishman were later additions, and hence dispensable; but one can certainly imagine them as second thoughts incorporated into the text by Shakespeare, who, processing words at postmodern speeds, subsequently forgot to alter the 'four' to 'six'. If they *were* additions, one possible motive would be to create audience resistance to the satire of national character, since they found themselves on the receiving end.

Given the respect of Brown, Mahood and Halio for the First Quarto as reflecting Shakespeare's compositional practice, one must wonder why they chose not to return to its consistent spelling of the names of major characters: Anthonio, Nerrissa and Launcelet (instead of the now conventional Antonio, Nerissa and Lancelot). 'Launcelet' could mean 'a little knife',[5] as in the modern medical 'lancet', and is not mysterious as a name for a 'wit-snapper' who is forever 'quarrelling with occasion', as Lorenzo complains; to use the Arthurian name 'Lancelot' merely in deference to editorial habit, on the other hand, may encourage unwarranted speculation into chivalric or mock-chivalric associations.

It does not matter much whether it was Shakespeare who hesitated between the forms 'Shyloch' (used only once) and

'Shylock', but he certainly juggled two spellings of Launcelet's patronymic, Jobbe and Gobbo. Surely this makes a difference, even in how we conceive of this figure. Launcelet only speaks of himself as Jobbe (Job, or Giobbe in Italian). As the type of undeserved suffering and temptation by the devil, this comic Job becomes another item in the play's complex series of Old Testament allusions, and an important counter to Shylock's self-identification with the cunning patriarch Jacob. 'Gobbo', however, appears only in relation to Launcelet's father. So it seems slightly misleading for Mahood to propose as Launcelet's original '*il Gobbo di Rialto*', the hunchback figure supporting the platform from which laws were promulgated, even if the Venetian Gobbo had the same function as the statue of Pasquino at Rome, of representing plebeian irreverence.

A modernised edition must lose partial sight of Shakespeare's speech habits, even if they appear in an apparatus. The First Quarto habitually uses 'I' for 'aye' (especially odd if capital I's are in short supply; see below), the already partly archaic 'cursey' for 'curtsey' (twice), the old 'flidge' for 'fledged', enhancing the flavour of the proverb about Jessica's leaving the nest, the old 'eche' for 'eke [out]', and the colourful 'shyddring' for 'shuddering' and 'phanges' for 'fangs'. (This last has left no trace in Mahood's and Brown's collations.) The First Quarto insists that the series 'oath', 'wroath' and 'moath' which mark Arragon's discomfiture is a rhyming series; it provides visual amusement from Shylock's joke about land rats, water rats and 'Pyrats', and a more complex charge from Gratiano's invective against Shylock, 'Not on thy soule: but on thy soule harsh Jew/thou makst thy knife keene'. This is not to say that the play's irrepressible stream of puns is treated in the 1600 Quarto with orthographical consistency. Portia's play on 'best/beast', Launcelet's on 'more' and 'the Moore', and Anthonio's 'my purse, my person', are all clarified as homonyms or near homonyms by the spelling; whereas Portia's self-evaluation ('the full summe of me/is sume of something') makes only an unuseful difficulty. As for the recurrent pun on 'gentle/Gentile', its layers of moral, class and racial complacency are never registered in the First Quarto by any shadow of the second word's difference from its phonetic twin.[6]

But if all the features just exemplified are worth the acquaintance of modern readers, as presumptive signs of the *compositional* process, they need to be distinguished from aspects of the 1600 Quarto that are clearly *compositorial* in origin, since they were caused by a shortage of type. From Portia's description of her French suitor, Mounsier le Boune, to the end of those mockings, again in Portia's scene with Morrocho when he makes his choice of the caskets, for the first half of her scene with Bassanio when he prepares to makes his, and in the great trial scene itself, a shortage of capital roman I's produces a disconcerting spray of capital italic I's and sometimes J's. In a few other scenes which involve Shylock, especially when he is being tormented by news of Jessica's 'unthrift' honeymoon, this phenomenon recurs. To normalise would run counter to the principles of a diplomatic text, even if those principles are rendered inconsistent by the translation of Elizabethan i to j. Not to normalise risks distracting the modern reader, but that distraction may be counterbalanced by noticing the frequency with which, and by whom, the first-person singular is used. It was especially Portia and her suitors who put a strain on the printer's supplies. (They were also strained by the Quarto's preference for spelling 'Aye' as 'I', and, of course, by the Elizabethan spelling of 'Jew' as 'Iew'.)

A parallel, but more subtle problem, is raised by the compositor's shortage of periods, and his sporadic substitution for them of question marks. This pattern begins in the scene where Portia initiates Nerrissa into her plan for disguising them as lawyer and clerk, when the 1600 Quarto has her say 'weele see our husbands/ before they thinke of us?', continues into Launcelet's bantering with Jessica and Lorenzo, and into the trial scene and its aftermath. Here the compositor's behaviour is more irritating, since he occasionally chooses a period when a question mark might be appropriate. See, for example, Shylock's response to Portia's statement, 'Then must the Jew be mercifull.' 'On what compulsion must I, tell me that.' On the other hand, if one imagines replacing all unexpected marks of interrogation with periods, it is not always clear on what authority one would do so. When Portia, still dressed as the Doctor, asks for Bassanio's ring ('and you in love shall not denie me this?') she is partly in the interrogative mode, and the same applies to Bassanio's reply, 'onely for this I pray you pardon

Introduction

me?' Likewise, can we tell whether the Duke's 'We all expect a gentle aunswere Jewe?' is a statement or a question? And the spray of question marks in Shylock's response and the stichomythia with Bassanio that follows can have the *visual* effect of heating up the rhetorical temperature of the scene, giving us the sense that Shylock's voice always rises at the end of a sentence. Still more to the point is Anthonio's comment on this exchange, which goes a long way towards justifying the compositor's expedient:

> I pray you think you question with the Jewe,
> ....
> you may as well use question with the Woolfe,
> why he hath made the Ewe bleake for the Lambe:
> ....
> You may as well doe any thing most hard
> as seeke to soften that then which what's harder:
> his Jewish hart?

This edition p. 90

The whole exchange is thereby marked as an act of interrogation, and the compositor's choice of punctuation after 'hart' seems somehow appropriate, especially after Shakespeare's decision to represent unintelligibility ('that then which what's harder') by syntactical and metrical unreadability. But, of course, Anthonio assumes that only one side in the exchange is human, and hence questioning; whereas the Quarto reminds us that Shylock, too, understands the clash between cultures as a series of futile inquiries.

This returns us to the question at the heart of all study of *The Merchant of Venice*, and to which the Quarto tradition of the play has an especially direct relation, as invoked by that misleading title-page: what is the play's final position on Shylock's would-be revenge? And even if it seems disproportionate, and appropriately deflected, what are we to think of the overt anti-Semitism of Launcelet the clown, the royal Merchant of Venice himself, and especially Gratiano, who in the trial scene becomes again the playboy-jester he had been in the opening scenes, but now a vicious one, snapping at Shylock like the dog to which he equates him? Or perhaps it would be better to pose the question not about the play's *final* position, which as elsewhere in Shakespeare seems to be more distressing to modern liberal readers than some of its earlier moments, but about its total representation of the Jewishness of Shylock and the responses it evokes in others. Was the Quarto intended to be bought and read as an anti-Semitic play? Or was it intended to be *purchased* as an anti-Semitic play, but one that could lure some of its readers into a more nuanced and anxious position? We need focus here only on what the Quarto text exclusively contributes to this issue. And central to that contribution is that feature already alluded to as a sign of its close relation to Shakespeare's manuscript: the alternation of the speech prefixes between 'Shylock' and 'Jew'. It is important to notice that whereas 'Shylock' is the commoner form in the early scenes between Shylock and Anthonio or Jessica, and is used exclusively in the scene where Tubal torments his kinsman with news of Jessica's extravagant honeymoon in Genoa (not only, surely, because there are two Jews present), in the later scenes as the catastrophe approaches the Quarto text, like the mood of the play, becomes *more* racially categorical. In the brief scene where Shylock torments Anthonio by his refusal to hear a word of negotiation, his own name has disappeared; and in the great trial scene itself, from 'Enter Shylocke' onwards his name appears fifteen times in the prefixes, whereas 'Jew' has nineteen appearances.[7] Whatever this means, it cannot mean that Shakespeare had not yet become secure in his decision as to what to name his tragic antagonist; nor is the *pattern* of variation explicable in terms of compositorial exigency.[8] Is it possible that the alternation in the playwright's responses deliberately mimics his characters? Or do they think like him?

Most readers will notice that the Duke begins his address by implying universal consensus ('*Shylocke* the world thinks, and I thinke so to,') and proceeds to encourage the spread of 'humaine gentlenes and love', but then moves to disparaging 'stubborne Turkes, and Tarters', and ends by invoking the play's most frequent and most reprehensible witticism: 'We all expect a gentle [Gentile] aunswere Jewe?' Despite the allure of the Shakespearean set speech, we may also notice the clash between Portia's invocation of mercy as 'the gentle raine from heaven' and her threatening deduction from her own principles:

therefore Jew,/though justice be thy plea, consider this,
that in the course of justice, none of us
should see salvation.

This edition, p. 94

The racial stereotype cuts in so harshly, and conflicts so obviously
with the 'us' of cultural dominance, that mercy comes to sound
more like justice after all. But what does it mean when the Quarto
text has Portia, as she embarks on her role as Balthazar, asking 'Is
your name *Shylocke*?' and when the natural answer, '*Shylocke* is my
name', is attributed in the margin only to a '*Jew*'? Of whose
consciousness does this silent conflict, never heard on stage, bear
witness? Given my assumption of the authorial presence in the 1600
Quarto, there is only one honest reply, and it is not a comforting
one. But how could Shakespeare have missed the irony of this
coincidence? And how does it compare, for self-consciousness,
with the ironies that accrue to those all-too-audible slippages in the
rhetoric of Portia and the Duke?

I shall leave these questions unanswered (in the spirit of Shylock's
response to the Duke's demand for a Gentile answer) while
considering the significance of the *later* Quarto tradition. Mahood
made a case for the independent interest of the Pavier Quarto of
1619, which had previously been discredited, either because of its
false '1600' imprint or because it is now clearly recognised as
derivative of Q1, or because of habitual faults attributed to one of
Jaggard's compositors. She detected instead 'the activity of a
sensitive and alert printer's reader', such as the corrections in the
names of two of Portia's suitors, and she gave its emendations
'more respect than they customarily receive' on the grounds that
they show how 'a Shakespeare play was read in 1619'. But as a
cultural event the Pavier Quarto is less interesting than the appearance of two subsequent Quartos, in 1637 and 1652. The 1619
Quarto was one of ten plays assembled by Thomas Pavier en route
to an aborted edition of Shakespeare's works. But the appearance of
a Quarto towards the end of the reign of Charles I is a more
provocative phenomenon. Caroline Quartos of Shakespeare are
rare, especially towards the end of the reign. The other instances
are *Romeo and Juliet* (1637), *Hamlet* (1636, 1637), and *Henry IV, Part
I* (1639), choices that might also deserve some historical interro-

[22]

gation. But whatever made those three plays appropriate for recirculation in the three years before Charles I's regime collapsed, it would not be surprising if the Belmont plot of *The Merchant of Venice* was attractive to the Caroline court. In both, romantic love is inseparable from royalism. Portia imagines the music which will accompany Bassanio's proper choice 'even as the flourish, when true subjects bowe/to a new crowned Monarch', and Bassanio responds to Portia's acceptance of him as 'her Lord, her governour, her King' by developing the metaphor in broader social terms:

> Maddam, you have bereft me of all words,
> onely my blood speakes to you in my vaines,
> and there is such confusion in my powers,
> as after some oration fairely spoke
> by a beloved Prince, there doth appeare
> among the buzzing pleased multitude.
> Where every somthing beeing blent together,
> turnes to a wild of nothing, save of joy
> exprest, and not exprest:
>
> This edition p. 78

This masque-like effacement of the problem of testing popular opinion (how can we really tell what the crowd is saying about the 'beloved Prince' when it all sounds like 'rhubarb'?) would mean as much or more in 1637 as it would in the last years of Elizabeth's reign.

There is, however, some disparity between these metaphors, and the fact that the arrogant Arragon *disqualifies* himself as a suitor by emphasising his high place in the class hierarchy; as he himself says:

> Because I will not jumpe with common spirits,
> And ranke me with the barbarous multitudes,
>
> This edition p. 68

he chooses the wrong casket. At least one director noticed the problem. In 1922, David Belasco adapted the play for the New York stage, and among other concessions to 'contemporary taste' he omitted the Arragon casket scene, and calmly transferred to Bassanio Arragon's complaint:[9]

> O that estates, degrees, and offices,
> were not deriv'd corruptly, and that cleare honour

were purchast by the merrit of the wearer,

....

How much low peasantry would then be gleaned
From the true seed of honour?

This edition p. 68

These sentiments were thus safely reclaimed for the American elite in the age of Edith Wharton.

For Mahood, the 'independent interest' of the 1637 Quarto consisted in its faithful return to the 1600 Quarto and its presentation, for the first time, of a list of 'Actors' Names'. Her edition does not note, however, that one of the British Library copies contains manuscript names of *actors* beside this list – actors not of the period of the first Charles, but of the second. Not all of these are legible, but one can learn that sometime during the Restoration the part of the Duke was played by Mr Freeman, that of Gratiano by Mr Bowman, of Lorenzo by Mr Mumford, of Shylock by Mr Sandford, and of Launcelet Gobbo by Mr Doggett. The significance of these last two names is considerable. At the Restoration the play was assigned to the Theatre Royal, but the standard wisdom is that it was never acted. Yet here we learn that Samuel Sandford, who was one of the principal actors at the Theatre Royal when the two houses joined in 1682, and who had a reputation as one of the finest tragic villains on the Restoration stage, played Shylock; while Thomas Doggett, once believed incorrectly to have been the first actor recorded as playing Shylock, is noted here in the role appropriate to *his* reputation as a clown.[10]

Finally, one has to wonder why modern editors of *The Merchant of Venice* pay no attention to the Fourth Quarto of 1652, published by William Leake Jr, the son of the Stationer William Leake.[11] Commonwealth quartos of Shakespeare's plays are more uncommon still than those of the Caroline period, and all three of them were Leake's productions, the other two being *Othello* and *King Lear* in 1655. The rights to all three were inherited by Leake very much earlier, in 1635, when his widowed mother turned over to him his Stationer father's copyrights. There was also an edition of *The Rape of Lucrece* in 1655, an unsurprising event given its republican argument and its pairing with John Quarles's *The Banishment of Tarquin*.[12] But what would an edition of the *Merchant*

[24]

of Venice have to say to readers in the years when the theatres were closed by parliamentary decree? There are aspects of Leake's practice that suggest he was aiming at royalist clients, the device of the crown on his title-pages referring to more than the name of his shop on Fleet Street. Among his other publications were Beaumont and Fletcher's *A King and No King*, James Shirley's *Grateful Servant*, and John Hart's *The Fort-Royal of Holy Scriptures* (1649), which, however, had nothing beyond its title to do with the constitutional issues of the day, and might reasonably have been reproached for misleading advertisement. On the other hand, Leake had also published John Clayton's *Topicks in the Laws of England* (1646), *without* his crown on the title-page, and accompanied by an ostentatiously republican dedication to Oliver St John and Oliver Cromwell.[13]

So the publisher at least was evenhanded, or perhaps merely business-like, with respect to the choice between royalism and republicanism. But there was another context more specific to *The Merchant of Venice*: the debate, beginning in the late 1640s but reaching a climax at the Whitehall Conference of 1656, as to whether the English under Oliver Cromwell's leadership should now put their money where their mouths were and officially readmit the Jews, as citizens with the right to practise their own religion.

The Whitehall Conference was the climax (and unfortunately a negative one) to a substantial philo-Semitic movement that had begun in James's reign for primarily theoretical and intellectual reasons (an intellectual interest in Mosaic law and rabbinical scholarship, a millenarian focus on the lost ten tribes of Israel), and that in the late 1640s had gathered strength from the Puritan revolution and some of *its* corollaries (a missionary zeal to bring about the conversion of the Jews, and a strategic support for toleration that would also benefit the Christian radical fringe).[14] In Cromwell himself there was probably also genuine interest in religious toleration as a necessary component of state reconstruction; and there were also economic motives percolating through this mixture, in which the United Provinces, or the Dutch Republic, played both a practical and an ideological role. As a consequence of their own revolt against Catholic Spain, the Dutch had established religious toleration, a principle enshrined in the 1579 Union of Utrecht. This included extremely liberal privileges for the Jews, whom the Dutch welcomed as contributors to trade and colonial expansionism.

Most importantly, there appeared during the English Revolution, and especially as the concept of Jewish readmission began to be publicly discussed, an explicit connection between philo-Semitism and republicanism, and between anti-Semitism and English royalism. When an earlier petition for readmission was submitted to the Council of State in 1649 from two Puritans, Joanna and Ebenezer Cartwright, mother and son, settled in Amsterdam,[15] its timing was provocative. The petition was presented and accepted on 5 January 1649, a few weeks before the beheading of Charles I. In the royalist newsletter *Mercurius Pragmaticus*, Clement Walker drew his own conclusions: 'No marvell that those which intend to crucifie their King, should shake hands with them that crucified their Saviour.' On 11 April, Thomason recorded his purchase of a pamphlet entitled *The Devilish Conspiracy, Hellish Treason, Heathenish Condemnation, and Damnable Murder, Committed and Executed by the Jewes, against the Anointed of the Lord,Christ their King*, the published text of a sermon delivered by Dr Warner, Bishop of Rochester, on 4 February, five days after the king's execution. This pamphlet constantly refers to 'Ch: their King', defines the Pharisees as Separatists (p. 4) and Presbyters (p. 9), and mentions the 'League and Covenant' (p. 13), thus making transparent the identity of the ancient Jews and the modern regicides. In 1652 the equally royalist James Howell published a translation of Jossipon's chronicle, which he entitled *The Wonderful And most deplorable History of the Latter Times of the Jews*, and prefaced it with a viciously anti-Semitic address to the mayor and sheriffs of London that self-evidently lobbied against readmission. But it also engaged in the constitutional issue. Howell's historical Jews, especially selected for divine punishment, deserved everything they got:

> Now, whosoever desires to make reserches into the grounds of these sad disasters, will finde it was their *seditious* proud spirits, their instable and stubborn *rebellious* hearts,

that left them scattered across the face of the earth (A3v; italics added). And since then, wrote Howell, 'this Nation is grown cowardly, and cunning even to a proverb':

much symbolizing in humour with some of the Apocalypticall
Zelots of these times, and bold expounders of Daniel, with the other
Prophets; whereby they use to sooth, or rather fool themselves into
some egregious fanaticall dotage, which nevertheless passeth among
them for an illumination. (A5v)

On the other side, Henry Jessey, who had experienced many
difficulties as a Nonconformist minister under Charles I and
Archbishop Laud, and who would later become a fund-raiser for
the indigent Jews in Jerusalem, published in 1656 *A Narrative of the
late Proceeds at White-Hall, concerning the Jews: Who had desired by
R. Manasses an Agent for them, they might return into England, and
Worship the God of their Fathers here in their Synagogues.* Jessey's
account claimed to be merely reportorial – and he certainly
reported fairly on the intense disagreements that were voiced
during the conference – but his own sympathies are clearly
apparent. The Whitehall Conference has been called, he explains,
because 'many Jews are now in very great streighs' (sic), those in
eastern Europe having been driven out by the Swedes and Cos-
sacks, and those in the Catholic countries of Europe and the
Spanish colonies being subject to religious oppression:

> if they are professed Jews, must wear a badge of it; & are exposed
> to many violencies, mocks, & cruelties; which to avoide, many
> dissemble themselves to be Roman Catholicks; and then if in any
> thing they appear Jewish, they forfeit goods, if not life also. (p. 3)

This line of argument was designed to appeal to a nation that had
recently fought a war against a 'popish' regime; and Jessey, citing
the commandment of Exodus, 23: 8, drew out the historical lesson
with some care:

> Many of the good people here, being persecuted in Queen Maries
> days, and under the Prelates since, have been kindly harboured as
> strangers in other Lands; and therefore should the more pity and
> harbour persecuted strangers, especially the persecuted Jews.

But he also presented the more practical commercial arguments
derived from observation of the Dutch Republic and its treatment
of mercantile foreigners.

In the same year that Howell published his disreputable production, William Leake published his Quarto edition of *The Merchant of*

Introduction

Venice, a reissue of the 1637 Quarto, but with a new title-page displaying his sign, the Crown. Unlike Howell's edition of Jossipon, there is no trace in this Fourth Quarto of any editorial intervention or framing. No *new* intervention, that is; for the title-page retains that untrustworthy and anti-Semitic information that the play is *about* 'the extreame crueltie of Shylocke the Jewe towards the sayd Merchant, in cutting a just pound of his flesh'. As a replica of the 1637 Quarto, however, which was itself faithfully based on the 1600 Quarto, the 1652 Quarto offered its readers the same troublesome fluctuations between 'Shylock' and 'Jew', both authorial and characterological.[16] And we know from the historical evidence that by this time the reading public included a broad range of influential figures, including Cromwell himself, who would have been ideologically capable, if not of identifying with Shylock, of understanding the dangerous force of stereotypification, of being shocked by the final judgement that Shylock must be baptised against his conscience, and of noticing the hypocrisies of the Christian crew.

To such a reader, Portia's scabrous witticisms on national character in her opening discussion with Nerrissa, and especially her dismissal of Morocho, 'Let all of his complexion choose me so', would align her with James Howell the royalist and xenophobe; whereas Shylock's appeal to a common humanity ('Hath not a Jewe eyes . . . if you pricke us doe we not bleede') and his attack on Christian culture for its tolerance of slavery, would align itself with the more radical rhetoric of the revolution. What is most interesting about the 1652 Quarto, finally, is that you simply cannot tell what 'the text itself' signifies in the context of the readmission debates. That the same play could mean different things to readers with different predilections was as true in the circumstances of the mid-seventeenth century as it is today.

NOTES AND REFERENCES

1. Jay Halio (ed.), *The Merchant of Venice* (Oxford: Clarendon Press, 1994), includes the 1600 title-page, but sandwiched between the critical and the textual introduction where its force goes unnoticed.
2. John Russell Brown, 'Compositors of *Hamlet* Q2 and *The Merchant of Venice*', *Studies in Bibliography*, 7 (1955), pp. 25–40.

3. Fredson Bowers, 'Seven or More Years?' in Clifford Leech and J.M.R. Margeson (eds), *Shakespeare 1971* (Toronto: University of Toronto Press, 1972), p. 58.

4. M.M. Mahood (ed.), *The Merchant of Venice* (Cambridge: Cambridge University Press, 1987; New Shakespeare edition), p. 173.

5. See Jürgen Schäfer, 'The Orthography of Proper Names in Modern-spelling Editions of Shakespeare', *Studies in Bibliography*, 23 (1970), pp. 1–19.

6. Q2, however acknowledges the difference when Gratiano praises Jessica as 'a Gentile and no Jew', an 'emendation' rejected by both Brown and Mahood.

7. Conceivably this habit caused the compositor's confusion in attributing Gratiano's gibe against Shylock, 'In christning shalt thou have two Godfathers', etc. to Shylock himself. That is, the manuscript may have read, 'Shy. in christning shalt thou have two godfathers', a reading not impossibly unmetrical given the feminine endings of surrounding lines.

8. The proposal that the compositors were led by a shortage of capital I's to switch speech prefixes *from* 'Jew' *to* 'Shylock' depends, as Halio (p. 89) points out, on the unverifiable assumption that the manuscript from which they were printing had 'Jew' throughout. In addition, this theory ignores the fact that one of the passages most heavily sprinkled with italic I's and J's in the text (from Shylock's statement of the 'certaine loathing' he bears Anthonio, to his appeal to the Duke, '*I* stand for judgement, aunswer, shall I have it',) also consistently uses the prefix 'Jewe'. If a shortage of capital I's was dictating the appearance of 'Shy'. it would certainly have happened here.

9. See *The Merchant of Venice . . . as arranged for the contemporary stage . . . with David Warfield In the Character of Shylock December 21, 1922* (New York, 1922).

10. On Sandford, see Tony Aston, *A Brief Supplement to Colley Cibber, esq; His Lives of the Late Famous Actors and Actresses* (London, 1747), p. 11: 'although not usually deem'd an Actor of the first Rank, yet the Characters allotted him were such, that none, besides, then, or since, ever topp'd . . . his Figure was despicable, (although his Energy was, by his voice and Action enforc'd with great soundness of Art, and Justice) – This Person acted strongly with his Face – and (as King Charles said) was the best Villain in the World'. Thomas Doggett's reputation for farcical parts led instead to his playing 'Chylock', 'a stock-jobbing Jew', in *The Jew of Venice*, the distorted version of the *Merchant* produced by George Granville, Viscount of Lansdowne, in

1701. Perversely, it seems to have been this role which led to the belief that Doggett played Shakespeare's Shylock, and played him as a comic character.

11. Brown remarks merely that 'some sheets of [the 1637] quarto were issued with a new title-page in 1652' (p. xx) and denies any 'special authority'. For Mahood its existence goes without comment.

12. *The rape of Lucrece: committed by Tarquin the sixt, and the remarkable judgments that befel him for it . . . whereunto is annexed, The banishment of Tarquin, or, The reward of lust, by J.O.* (London: printed by J.G. for John Stafford and William Gilbertson, 1655).

13. John Clayton, *Topicks in the Laws of England* (London, 1646), A3v: 'I shall not need much to implore your protections who cherish every sparke appears for the publike. The Lord make you ride on with good luck for the rejoynting again his Majesty, and the great Councel of England, the Head and the Members, and that the Laws, one part (whereof is priviledge of Parliament) may be maintained and duly executed, for as Bracton saith, *Parum est jus in Civitate esse, nisi sint qui possint jura gerere*, which if I mistake not, is a main ground of this bloudie Quarrell, which God end in due time, and in the accomplishment of Peace and Truth.'

14. For a useful account of this movement, see David Katz, *Philo-Semitism and the Readmission of the Jews to England 1603–1655* (Oxford: Oxford University Press, 1982).

15. J. Cartenright and E. Cartwright, *The Petition of the Jewes for the repealing of the Act of Parliament for their banishment out of England. Presented to His Excellency and the Generall Council of Officers on Fryday, Jan. 5, 1648.*

16. The anomalies in the speech prefixes were retained while those in punctuation (the unwanted question marks) were removed.

Select Bibliography

Brown, John Russell, 'Compositors of *Hamlet* Q2 and *The Merchant of Venice*, SB 7 (1955), pp. 25–40.

Brown, John Russell (ed.), *The Merchant of Venice* (London: Methuen, 1966).

Cloud, Random (Randall McLeod), 'The Marriage of Good and Bad Quartos' *Shakespeare Quarterly*, vol. 33, no. 4 (1982), pp. 421–31.

Evans, G. Blakemore (textual ed.), *The Riverside Shakespeare* (Boston: Houghton Mifflin, 1974).

Goldberg, Jonathan, 'Textual Properties', *Shakespeare Quarterly*, vol. 37, no. 2 (Summer 1986), pp. 213–17.

Grazia, Margreta de, *Shakespeare Verbatim* (Oxford: Oxford University Press, 1991).

Grazia, Margreta de and Peter Stallybrass, 'The Materiality of the Shakespearean Text', *Shakespeare Quarterly*, vol. 44, no. 3 (Fall 1993), pp. 255–83.

Halio, Jay L. (ed.), *The Merchant of Venice* (Oxford: Clarendon Press, 1994).

Hinman, Charlton (ed.) *The First Folio of Shakespeare* (New York: Norton, 1968).

Ioppolo, Grace, *Revising Shakespeare* (Cambridge, Mass.: Harvard University Press, 1991).

Mahood, M.M. (ed.), *The Merchant of Venice* (Cambridge: Cambridge University Press, 1987).

Merchant, W.M. (ed.), *The Merchant of Venice* (London: Penguin, 1981).

Wells, Stanley and Gary Taylor with John Jowett and William Montgomery, *William Shakespeare: A Textual Companion* (Oxford: Clarendon Press, 1987).

Textual History

T H I S play was initially published in 1600, in Quarto format, with
the following title-page:

The most excellent

Historie of the *Merchant*
of Venice.

With the extreme crueltie of *Shylocke* the Jewe
towards the sayd Merchant, in cutting a just pound
of his flesh: and the obtayning of Portia
by the choyse of three
chests.

As it hath beene divers times acted by the Lord
Chamberlaine his Servants.

Written   by   William Shakespeare.

AT   LONDON,

Printed by J.R. for Thomas Heyes,
and are to be sold in Paules Church-yard, at the
signe of the Green Dragon.
1600.

This First Quarto is a very fine text, showing signs of being closer
to Shakespeare's own manuscript than a prompt book, and possibly

printed directly from the holograph. Three copies are held at the British Library. A Second Quarto, falsely dated 1600, was printed in 1619 by William Jaggard for Thomas Pavier. It is clearly a reprint of the First Quarto. The 1623 Folio text was also based on the First Quarto, with a few emendations. Quarto texts were also published in 1637 (by M.P. for Laurence Hayes) and in 1652 (printed by William Leake). Facsimiles were published by E.W. Ashbee (p.p., 1865, 1870), and by C. Praetorius, in the Shakspere-Quarto Facsimiles series (London, 1887), with a foreword by Frederick Furnivall, and act and scene division added in the margins. A facsimile of the Huntington Library copy of the 1600 Quarto appeared in Michael Allen and Kenneth Muir (eds), *Shakespeare's Plays in Quarto* (Berkeley and Los Angeles, 1981); and it was used as the copy-text for the New Arden edition (ed. John Russell Brown, 1955, repr. 1961), the New Cambridge edition, ed. M.M. Mahood (Cambridge, 1987), and the World's Classics edition, ed. Jay Halio (Oxford and New York, 1994). This edition is prepared from British Library C.112.g.11, with C.34.k.22 used for the defective lines on p. 90.

The most excellent

Historie of the *Merchant* *of Venice*.

VVith the extreame crueltie of *Shylocke* the Iewe
towards the fayd Merchant, in cutting a iuſt pound
of his fleſh: and the obtayning of *Portia*
by the choyſe of three
cheſts.

As it hath beene diuers times aɛted by the Lord
Chamberlaine his Seruants.

Written by William Shakeſpeare.

AT LONDON,
Printed by *I. R.* for Thomas Heyes,
and are to be ſold in Paules Church-yard, at the
ſigne of the Greene Dragon.
1 6 0 0.

THE MOST EXCELLENT HISTORIE OF
The Merchant of Venice

The comicall History of the Mer-
chant of Venice.

Enter *Anthonio, Salaryno,* and *Salanio.*

An. In sooth I know not why I am so sad,
It wearies me, you say it wearies you;
But how I caught it, found it, or came by it,
What stuffe tis made of, whereof it is borne,
I am to learne: and such a want-wit sadnes
     makes of mee,
That I have much adoe to know my selfe.
Salarino. Your minde is tossing on the Ocean,
There where your Argosies with portlie sayle
Like Signiors and rich Burgars on the flood,
Or as it were the Pageants of the sea,
Doe over-peere the petty traffiquers
That cursie to them do them reverence
As they flie by them with theyr woven wings.
Salanio. Beleeve mee sir, had I such venture forth,
The better part of my affections would
Be with my hopes abroad. I should be still
Plucking the grasse to know where sits the wind,
Piring in Maps for ports, and peers and rodes:

[37]

And every object that might make me feare
Mis-fortune to my ventures, out of doubt
Would make me sad.

    Salar. My wind cooling my broth,
would blow me to an ague when I thought
what harme a winde too great might doe at sea.
I should not see the sandie howre-glasse runne
But I should thinke of shallowes and of flatts,
And see my wealthy *Andrew* docks in sand
Vayling her high top lower then her ribs
To kisse her buriall; should I goe to Church
And see the holy edifice of stone
And not bethinke me straight of dangerous rocks,
which touching but my gentle vessels side
would scatter all her spices on the streame,
Enrobe the roring waters with my silkes,
And in a word, but even now worth this,
And now worth nothing. Shall I have the thought
To thinke on this, and shall I lack the thought
That such a thing bechaunc'd would make me sad?
But tell me not, I know *Anthonio*
Is sad to thinke upon his merchandize.

    Anth. Beleeve me no, I thanke my fortune for it
My ventures are not in one bottome trusted,
Nor to one place; nor is my whole estate
Upon the fortune of this present yeere:
Therefore my merchandize makes me not sad.

    Sola. Why then you are in love.

    Anth. Fie, fie.

    Sola. Not in love neither: then let us say you are sad
Because you are not merry; and twere as easie
For you to laugh and leape, and say you are merry
Because you are not sad. Now by two-headed *Janus*,
Nature hath framd strange fellowes in her time:
Some that will evermore peepe through their eyes,
And laugh like Parrats at a bagpyper.
And other of such vinigar aspect,

That theyle not shew theyr teeth in way of smile
Though *Nestor* sweare the jest be laughable.

Enter Bassanio, Lorenso, and Gratiano.

Sola. Here comes *Bassanio* your most noble kinsman,
Gratiano, and *Lorenso.* Faryewell,
We leave you now with better company.
    Sala. I would have staid till I had made you merry,
If worthier friends had not prevented me.
    Anth. Your worth is very deere in my regard.
I take it your owne busines calls on you,
And you embrace th'occasion to depart.
    Sal. Good morrow my good Lords.
    Bass. Good signiors both when shal we laugh? say, when?
You grow exceeding strange: must it be so?
    Sal. Weele make our leysures to attend on yours.

Exeunt Salarino, and Solanio.

Lor. My Lord *Bassanio*, since you have found *Anthonio*
We two will leave you, but at dinner time
I pray you have in minde where we must meete.
    Bass. I will not faile you.
    Grat. You looke not well signior *Anthonio,*
You have too much respect upon the world:
They loose it that doe buy it with much care,
Beleeve me you are mervailously changd.
    Ant. I hold the world but as the world *Gratiano,*
A stage, where every man must play a part,
And mine a sad one.
    Grati. Let mee play the foole,
With mirth and laughter let old wrinckles come,
And let my liver rather heate with wine
Then my hart coole with mortifying grones.
Why should a man whose blood is warme within,
Sit like his grandsire, cut in Alablaster?
Sleepe when he wakes? and creepe into the Jaundies
By beeing peevish? I tell thee what *Anthonio,*

[39]

I love thee, and tis my love that speakes:
There are a sort of men whose visages
Doe creame and mantle like a standing pond,
And doe a wilful stilnes entertaine,
With purpose to be drest in an opinion
Of wisedome, gravitie, profound conceit,
As who should say, I am sir Oracle,
And when I ope my lips, let no dogge barke.
O my *Anthonio* I doe know of these
That therefore onely are reputed wise
For saying nothing; when I am very sure
If they should speake, would almost dam those eares
which hearing them would call their brothers fooles,
Ile tell thee more of this another time.
But fish not with this melancholy baite
For this foole gudgin, this opinion:
Come good *Lorenso*, faryewell a while,
Ile end my exhortation after dinner.

Loren. Well, we will leave you then till dinner time.
I must be one of these same dumbe wise men,
For *Gratiano* never lets me speake.

Gra. Well keepe me company but two yeeres moe
Thou shalt not know the sound of thine owne tongue.

An. Far you well, Ile grow a talker for this geare.

Gra. Thanks yfaith, for silence is onely commendable
In a neates togue dried, and a mayde not vendable.   *Exeunt.*

An. It is that any thing now.

Bass. *Gratiano* speakes an infinite deale of nothing more then any man in all Venice, his reasons are as two graines of wheate hid in two bushels of chaffe: you shall seeke all day ere you finde them and when you have them, they are not worth the search.

An. Well, tell me now what Lady is the same
To whom you swore a secrete pilgrimage
That you to day promisd to tell me of.

Bass. Tis not unknowne to you *Anthonio*
How much I have disabled mine estate,

the Merchant of Venice

By something showing a more swelling port
Then my faint meanes would graunt continuance:
Nor doe I now make mone to be abridg'd
From such a noble rate, but my cheefe care
Is to come fairely of from the great debts
wherein my time something too prodigall
Hath left me gagd: to you *Anthonio*
I owe the most in money and in love,
And from your love I have a warrantie
To unburthen all my plots and purposes
How to get cleere of all the debts I owe.

An. I pray you good *Bassanio* let me know it,
And if it stand as you your selfe still doe,
within the eye of honour, be assurd
My purse, my person, my extreamest meanes
Lie all unlockt to your occasions.

Bass. In my schoole dayes, when I had lost one shaft,
I shot his fellow of the selfe same flight
The selfe same way, with more advised watch
To finde the other forth, and by adventuring both,
I oft found both: I urge this child-hood proofe
Because what followes is pure innocence.
I owe you much, and like a wilfull youth
That which I owe is lost, but if you please
To shoote another arrow that selfe way
which you did shoote the first, I doe not doubt,
As I will watch the ayme or to find both,
Or bring your latter hazzard bake againe,
And thankfully rest debter for the first.

An. You know me well, and heerein spend but time
To wind about my love with circumstance,
And out of doubt you doe me now more wrong
In making question of my uttermost
Then if you had made waste of all I have:
Then doe but say to me what I should doe
That in your knowledge may by me be done,
And I am prest unto it: therefore speake.

[41]

Bass. In *Belmont* is a Lady richly left,
And she is faire, and fairer then that word,
Of wondrous vertues, sometimes from her eyes
I did receave faire speechlesse messages:
Her name is *Portia*, nothing undervallewd
To *Catos* daughter, *Brutus Portia*,
Nor is the wide world ignorant of her worth,
For the foure winds blow in from every coast
Renowned sutors, and her sunny locks
Hang on her temples like a golden fleece,
which makes her seat of *Belmont Cholchos* strond,
And many *Jasons* come in quest of her.
O my *Anthonio*, had I but the meanes
To hold a rivall place with one of them,
I have a mind presages me such thrift
That I should questionlesse be fortunate.

Anth. Thou knowst that all my fortunes are at sea,
Neither have I money, nor commoditie
To raise a present summe, therefore goe forth
Try what my credite can in Venice doe,
That shall be rackt even to the uttermost
To furnisht thee to *Belmont* to faire *Portia*.
Goe presently enquire and so will I
where money is, and I no question make
To have it of my trust, or for my sake.   *Exeunt.*

Enter *Portia* with her wayting woman *Nerrissa*.

Portia. By my troth *Nerrissa*, my little body is awearie of this
          great world.
Ner. You would be sweet Madam, if your miseries were in
the same aboundance as your good fortunes are: and yet for
ought I see, they are as sicke that surfeite with too much, as
they that starve with nothing; it is no meane happines
therfore to be seated in the meane, superfluitie comes sooner
by white haires, but competencie lives longer.
Portia. Good sentences, and well pronounc'd.
Ner. They would be better if well followed.

[42]

Portia. If to do were as easie as to know what were good to do, Chappels had beene Churches, and poore mens cottages Princes Pallaces, it is a good divine that followes his owne instructions, I can easier teach twentie what were good to be done, then to be one of the twentie to follow mine owne teaching: the braine may devise lawes for the blood, but a hote temper leapes ore a colde decree, such a hare is madness the youth, to skippe ore the meshes of good counsaile the cripple; but this reasoning is not in the fashion to choose mee a husband, ô mee the word choose, I may neyther choose who I would, nor refuse who I dislike, so is the will of a lyving daughter curbd by the will of a deade father: is it not harde *Nerrissa*, that I cannot choose one, nor refuse none.

Ner. Your Father was ever vertuous, and holy men at theyr death have good inspirations, therefore the lottrie that he hath devised in these three chests of gold, silver, and leade, whereof who chooses his meaning chooses you, will no doubt never be chosen by any rightlie, but one who you shall rightly love: But what warmth is there in your affection towardes any of these Princelie suters that are already come?

Por. I pray thee over-name them, and as thou namest them, I will describe them, and according to my description levell at my affection.

Ner. First there is the Neopolitane Prince.

Por. I thats a colt indeede, for he doth nothing but talke of his horse, & he makes it a great appropriation to his owne good parts that he can shoo him himselfe: I am much afeard my Ladie his mother plaid false with a Smyth.

Ner. Than is there the Countie Palentine.

Por. Hee doth nothing but frowne (as who should say, & you will not have me, choose, he heares merry tales and smiles not, I feare hee will proove the weeping Phylosopher when hee growes old, beeing so full of unmannerly sadnes in his youth.) I had rather be married to a deaths head with a bone in his mouth, then to eyther of these: God defend me from these two.

Ner. How say you by the French Lord, Mounsier *Le Boune*?

Por. God made him, and therefore let him passe for a man, in truth I knowe it is a sinne to be a mocker, but hee, why hee hath a horse better then the Neopolitans, a better bad habite of frowning then the Count Palentine, he is every man in no man, if a Trassell sing, he falls straght a capring, he will fence with his owne shadow. If I should marry him, I should marry twenty husbands: if hee would despise me, *I* would forgive him, for if he love me to madnes, *I* shall never requite him.

Ner. What say you then to Fauconbridge, the young Barron of England?

Por. You know *I* say nothing to him, for hee understands not me, nor *I* him: he hath neither Latine, French, nor *I*talian, & you will come into the Court and sweare that *I* have a poore pennieworth in the English: he is a proper mans picture, but alas who can converse with a dumbe show? how odly hee is suted, *I* thinke he bought his doublet in *I*talie, his round hose in Fraunce, his bonnet in Germanie, and his behaviour every where.

Nerrissa. What thinke you of the Scottish Lorde his neighbour?

Portia. That hee hath a neyghbourlie charitie in him, for hee borrowed a boxe of the eare of the Englishman, and swore hee would pay him againe when he was able: *I* think the Frenchman became his suretie, and seald under for another.

Ner. How like you the young Germaine, the Duke of Saxonies nephew?

Por. Very vildlie in the morning when hee is sober, and most vildly in the afternoone when he is drunke: when he is best, he is a little worse then a man, & when he is worst he is little better then a beast, and the worst fall that ever fell, I hope I shall make shift to goe without him.

Ner. Yf hee shoulde offer to choose, and choose the right Casket, you should refuse to performe your Fathers will, if you should refuse to accept him.

Portia. Therefore for feare of the worst, *I* pray thee set a deepe glasse of Reynishe wine on the contrarie Casket, for if the devill be within, and that temptation without, I knowe hee will choose it. I will doe any thing *Nerrissa* ere *I* will be married to a spunge.

Nerrissa. You neede not feare Ladie the having anie of these Lords, they have acquainted me with theyr determinations, which is indeede to return to theyr home, and to trouble you with no more sute, unlesse you may be wonne by some other sort then your Fathers imposition, depending on the Caskets.

Por. If I live to be as old as Sibilla, *I* will die as chast as Diana, unlesse I be obtained by the maner of my Fathers will: I am glad this parcell of wooers are so reasonable, for there is not one among them but *I* doate on his very absence: & *I* pray God graunt them a faire departure.

Nerrissa. Doe you not remember Lady in your Fathers time, a Venecian a Scholler & a Souldiour that came hether in companie of the Marquesse of Mountferrat?

Portia. Yes, yes, it was *Bassanio*, as I thinke so was he calld.

Ner. True maddam, hee of all the men that ever my foolish eyes look'd upon, was the best deserving a fair Ladie.

Portia. I remember him well, and *I* remember him worthie of thy prayse. How nowe, what newes?

Enter a Servingman.

Ser. The foure strangers seeke for you maddam to take theyr leave: and there is a fore-runner come from a fift, the Prince of *Moroco*, who brings word the Prince his Maister will be heere to night.

Por. Yf *I* could bid the fift welcome with so good hart as *I* can bid the other foure farewell, *I* should bee glad of his approch: if he have the condition of a Saint, and the complexion of a devill, I had rather he should shrive mee then wive mee. Come *Nerrissa*, sirra goe before: whiles we shut the gate upon one wooer, another knocks at the doore.   *Exeunt*

Enter *Bassanio* with *Shylocke* the Jew.

Shy. Three thousand ducates, well.

Bas. I sir, for three months.

Shy. For three months, well.

Bass. For the which as I told you,
    Anthonio shalbe bound.

Shy. Anthonio shall become bound, well.

Bass. May you sted me? Will you pleasure me?
    Shall *I* know your aunswere.

Shy. Three thousand ducats for three months,
    and *Anthonio* bound.

Bass. Your aunswere to that.

Shy. Anthonio is a good man.

Bass. Have you heard any imputation to the contrary.

Shylocke. Ho no, no, no, no: my meaning in saying hee is a good man, is to have you understand mee that hee is sufficient, yet his meanes are in supposition: hee hath an Argosie bound to Tripolis, another to the Indies, I understand moreover upon the Ryalta, hee hath a third at Mexico, a fourth for England, and other ventures he hath squandred abroade, but ships are but boordes, Saylers but men, there be land rats, and water rats, water theeves, and land theeves, *I* meane Pyrats, and then there is the perrill of waters, windes, and rockes: the man is notwithstanding sufficient, three thousand ducats, *I* thinke *I* may take his bond.

Bas. Be assurd you may.

Jew. I will be assurd *I* may: and that *I* may be assured, *J* will bethinke mee, may *I* speake with *Anthonio*?

Bass. Yf it please you to dine with us.

Jew. Yes, to smell porke, to eate of the habitation which your Prophet the Nazarit conjured the devill into: *I* wil buy with you, sell with you, talke with you, walke with you, and so following: but *I* will not eate with you, drinke with you, nor pray with you. What newes on the Ryalto, who is he comes heere?

Enter *Anthonio*.

Bass. This is signior *Anthonio.*

Jew. How like a fawning publican he lookes.
I hate him for he is a Christian:
But more, for that in low simplicitie
He lends out money gratis, and brings downe
The rate of usance heere with us in Venice.
Yf I can catch him once upon the hip,
I will feede fat the auncient grudge I beare him.
He hates our sacred Nation, and he rayles
Even there where Merchants most doe congregate
On me, my bargaines, and my well-wone thrift,
Which he calls interrest: Cursed be my Trybe
if I forgive him.

Bass. *Shyloch*, doe you heare.

Shyl. J am debating of my present store,
And by the neere gesse of my memorie
I cannot instantly raise up the grosse
Of full three thousand ducats: what of that,
Tuball a wealthy Hebrew of my Tribe
Will furnish me; but soft, how many months
Doe you desire? Rest you faire good signior,
Your worship was the last man in our mouthes.

An. *Shylocke*, albeit I neither lend nor borrow
By taking nor by giving of excesse,
Yet to supply the ripe wants of my friend,
Ile breake a custome: is hee yet possest
How much ye would?

Shy. J, I, three thousand ducats.

Ant. And for three months.

Shyl. I had forgot, three months, you told me so.
Well then, your bond: and let me see, but heare you,
Me thoughts you said, you neither lend nor borrow
Upon advantage.

Ant. I doe never use it.

Shy. When *Jacob* grazd his Uncle *Labans* Sheepe,
This *Jacob* from our holy *Abram* was
(As his wise mother wrought in his behalfe)

[47]

The third possesser; *I*, he was the third.
   Ant. And what of him, did he take interrest?
   Shyl. No, not take interest, not as you would say
Directly intrest, marke what *Jacob* did,
When Laban and himselfe were compremyzd
That all the eanelings which were streakt and pied
Should fall as *Jacobs* hier, the Ewes being ranck
In end of Autume turned to the Rammes,
And when the worke of generation was
Betweene these wolly breeders in the act,
The skilful sheepheard pyld me certaine wands,
And in the dooing of the deede of kind
He stuck them up before the fulsome Ewes,
Who then conceaving, did in eaning time
Fall party-coulord lambs, and those were *Jacobs*.
This was a way to thrive, and he was blest:
And thrift is blessing if men steale it not.
   An. This was a venture sir that *Jacob* servd for.
A thing not in his power to bring to passe,
But swayd and fashiond by the hand of heaven.
Was this inserted to make interrest good?
Or is your gold and silver ewes and rammes?
   Shyl. I cannot tell, I make it breede as fast,
      but note me signior.
   Anth. Marke you this *Bassanio*,
The devill can cite Scripture for his purpose,
An evill soule producing holy witnes
Is like a villaine with a smiling cheeke,
A goodly apple rotten at the hart.
O what a goodly out-side falshood hath.
   Shy. Three thousand ducats, tis a good round summe.
Three months from twelve, then let me see the rate.
   Ant. Well *Shylocke*, shall we be beholding to you?
   Shyl. Signior *Anthonio*, manie a time and oft
In the Ryalto you have rated me
About my moneyes and my usances:
Still have I borne it with a patient shrug,

(For suffrance is the badge of all our Trybe)
You call me misbeleever, cut-throate dog,
And spet upon my Jewish gaberdine,
And all for use of that which is mine owne.
Well then, it now appeares you neede my helpe:
Goe to then, you come to me and you say,
Shylocke, we would have moneyes, you say so:
You that did voyde your rume upon my beard,
And foote me as you spurne a stranger curre
Over your threshold, moneyes is your sute.
What should I say to you? Should I not say
Hath a dog money? is it possible
A curre can lend three thousand ducats? or
Shall I bend low, and in a bond-mans key
With bated breath, and whispring humblenes
Say this: Faire sir, you spet on me on Wednesday last,
You spurnd me such a day another time,
You calld me dogge: and for these curtesies
Ile lend you thus much moneyes.

    Ant. J am as like to call thee so againe,
To spet on thee againe, to spurne thee to.
Yf thou wilt lend this money, lend it not
As to thy friends, for when did friendship take
A breede for barraine mettaile of his friend?
But lend it rather to thine enemie,
Who if he breake, thou maist with better face
Exact the penaltie.

    Shy. Why looke you how you storme,
I would be friends with you, and have your love,
Forget the shames that you have staind me with,
Supply your present wants, and take no doyte
Of usance for my moneyes, and youle not heare mee,
        this is kinde I offer.

    Bass. This were kindnesse.

    Shyl. This kindnesse will I showe,
Goe with me to a Notarie, seale me there
Your single bond, and in a merrie sport

if you repay me not on such a day
in such a place, such summe or summes as are
exprest in the condition, let the forfaite
be nominated for an equall pound
of your faire flesh, to be cut off and taken
in what part of your bodie pleaseth me.

Ant. Content infaith, yle seale to such a bond,
And say there is much kindnes in the Jew.

Bass. You shall not seale to such a bond for me,
Ile rather dwell in my necessitie.

An. Why feare not man, I will not forfaite it,
within these two months, thats a month before
this bond expires, I doe expect returne
of thrice three times the valew of this bond.

Shy. O father Abram, what these Christians are,
Whose owne hard dealings teaches them suspect
the thoughts of others: Pray you tell me this,
if he should breake his day what should I gaine
by the exaction of the forfeyture?
A pound of mans flesh taken from a man,
is not so estimable, profitable neither
as flesh of Muttons, Beefes, or Goates, I say
To buy his favour, I extend this friendship,
Yf he wil take it, so, if not adiew,
And for my love I pray you wrong me not.

An. Yes *Shylocke*, I will seale unto this bond.

Shy. Then meete me forthwith at the Noteries,
Give him direction for this merry bond
And I will goe and purse the ducats straite,
See to my house left in the fearefull gard
Of an unthriftie knave: and presently
Ile be with you.   *Exit.*

An. Hie thee gentle Jewe. The Hebrew will turne
Christian, he growes kinde.

Bassa. I like not faire termes, and a villaines minde.

An. Come on, in this there can be no dismay,
My ships come home a month before the day.

[50]

Enter *Morochus* a tawnie Moore all in white, and three
or foure followers accordingly, with *Portia*,
Nerrissa, and their traine.

Morocho. Mislike me not for my complexion,
The shadowed liverie of the burnisht sunne,
To whom I am a neighbour, and neere bred.
Bring me the fayrest creature North-ward borne,
Where *Phoebus* fire scarce thawes the ysicles,
And let us make incyzion for your love,
To prove whose blood is reddest, his or mine.
I tell thee Lady this aspect of mine
Hath feard the valiant, (by my love I sweare)
The best regarded Virgins of our Clyme
Have lov'd it to: I would not change this hue,
Except to steale your thoughts my gentle Queene.
    Portia. In termes of choyse I am not soly led
By nice direction of a maydens eyes:
Besides, the lottrie of my destenie
Barrs me the right of voluntary choosing:
But if my Father had not scanted me,
And hedgd me by his wit to yeeld my selfe
His wife, who winnes me by that meanes I told you,
Your selfe (renowned Prince) than stoode as faire
As any commer I have look'd on yet
For my affection.
    Mor. Even for that I thanke you,
Therefore I pray you leade me to the Caskets
To try my fortune: By this Symitare
That slewe the Sophy, and a Persian Prince
That wone three fields of Sultan Solyman,
I would ore-stare the sternest eyes that looke:
Out-brave the hart most daring on the earth:
Pluck the young sucking Cubs from the she Beare,
Yea, mock the Lyon when a rores for pray
To win the Lady. But alas, the while

[51]

If *Hercules* and *Lychas* play at dice
Which is the better man, the greater throw
May turne by fortune from the weaker hand:
So is *Alcides* beaten by his rage,
And so may I, blind Fortune leading me
Misse that which one unworthier may attaine,
And die with greeving.

 Portia. You must take your chaunce,
And eyther not attempt to choose at all,
Or sweare before you choose, if you choose wrong
Never to speake to Lady afterward
In way of marriage, therefore be advis'd.

 Mor. Nor will not, come bring me unto my chaunce.

 Portia. First forward to the temple, after dinner
Your hazard shall be made.

 Mor. Good fortune then,
To make me blest or cursed'st among men.

            Exeunt.

    Enter the Clowne alone.

 Clowne. Certainely, my conscience will serve me to runne
from this Jewe my Maister: the fiend is at mine elbow, and
tempts me, saying to me, *Jobbe, Launcelet Jobbe,* good
Launcelet, or good *Jobbe,* or good *Launcelet Jobbe,* use your
legges, take the start, runne away, my conscience sayes no;
take heede honest *Launcelet,* take heede honest *Jobbe,* or as
afore-saide honest *Launcelet Jobbe,* doe not runne, scorne
running with thy heeles; well, the most coragious fiend bids
me packe, *fia* sayes the fiend, away sayes the fiend, for the
heavens rouse up a brave minde sayes the fiend, and runne;
well, my conscience hanging about the necke of my heart,
sayes very wisely to mee: my honest friend *Launcelet* beeing
an honest mans sonne, or rather an honest womans sonne,
for indeede my Father did something smacke, something
grow to; he had a kinde of tast; well, my conscience sayes
Launcelet bouge not, bouge sayes the fiend, bouge not sayes
my conscience, conscience say I you counsaile wel, fiend say I

       [52]

you counsaile well, to be ruld by my conscience, I should stay with the Jewe my Maister, (who God blesse the marke) is a kinde of devill; and to runne away from the Jewe I should be ruled by the fiend, who saving your reverence is the devill himselfe: certainely the Jewe is the very devill incarnation, and in my conscience, my conscience is but a kinde of hard conscience, to offer to counsaile mee to stay with the Jewe; the fiend gives the more friendly counsaile: I will runne fiend, my heeles are at your commaundement, I will runne.

Enter old Gobbo with a basket.

Gobbo. Maister young-man, you I pray you, which is the way to Maister Jewes?

Launcelet. O heavens, this is my true begotten Father, who being more then sand blinde, high gravell blinde, knowes me not, I will try confusions with him.

Gobbo. Maister young Gentleman, I pray you which is the way to Maister Jewes.

Launcelet. Turne up on your right hand at the next turning, but at the next turning of all on your left; marry at the very next turning turne of no hand, but turne downe indirectly to the Jewes house.

Gobbo. Be Gods sonties twill be a hard way to hit, can you tell mee whether one *Launcelet* that dwels with him, dwell with him or no.

Launcelet. Talke you of young Maister *Launcelet*, marke mee nowe, nowe will I raise the waters; talke you of young Maister *Launcelet*.

Gobbo. No Maister sir, but a poore mans Sonne, his Father though I say't is an honest exceeding poore man, and God bee thanked well to live.

Launce. Well, let his Father be what a will, wee talke of young Maister *Launcelet*.

Gob. Your worships friend and *Launcelet* sir.

Launce. But I pray you *ergo* olde man, *ergo* I beseech you, talke you of young Maister *Launcelet*.

Gob. Of *Launcelet* ant please your maistership.

Launce. Ergo Maister *Launcelet*, talke not of maister *Launcelet* Father, for the young Gentleman according to fates and destenies, and such odd sayings, the sisters three, and such braunches of learning, is indeede deceased, or as you would say in plaine termes, gone to heaven.

Gobbo. Marry God forbid, the boy was the very staffe of my age, my very prop.

Launcelet. Doe I looke like a cudgell or a hovell post, a staffe, or a prop: doe you know me Father.

Gobbo. Alacke the day, I knowe you not young Gentleman, but I pray you tell mee, is my boy G O D rest his soule alive or dead.

Launcelet. Doe you not know me Father.

Gobbo. Alack sir I am sand blind, I know you not.

Launcelet. Nay, in deede if you had your eyes you might fayle of the knowing mee: it is a wise Father that knowes his owne childe. Well, olde man, I will tell you newes of your sonne, give mee your blessing, trueth will come to light, muder cannot bee hidde long, a mannes Sonne may, but in the end trueth will out.

Gobbo. Pray you sir stand up, I am sure you are not *Launcelet* my boy.

Launce. Pray you let's have no more fooling, about it, but give mee your blessing: I am *Launcelet* your boy that was, your sonne that is, your child that shall be.

Gob. I cannot thinke you are my sonne.

Launce. I know not what I shall think of that: but I am *Launcelet* the Jewes man, and I am sure *Margerie* your wife is my mother.

Gob. Her name is *Margerie* in deede, ile be sworne if thou bee *Launcelet*, thou art mine owne flesh and blood: Lord worshipt might he be, what a beard hast thou got; thou hast got more haire on thy chinne, then Dobbin my philhorse hase on his taile.

Launce. It should seeme then that Dobbins taile growes backward. I am sure hee had more haire of his taile then I have of my face when I lost saw him.

Gob. Lord how art thou changd: how doost thou and thy Master agree, I have brought him a present; how gree you now?

Launce. Well, well, but for mine owne part, as I have set up my rest to runne away, so I will not rest till I have runne some ground; my Maister's a very Jewe, give him a present, give him a halter, I am famisht in his service. You may tell every finger I have with my ribs: Father I am glad you are come, give me your present to one Maister *Bassanio*, who in deede gives rare newe Lyvories, if I serve not him, I will runne as farre as God has any ground. O rare fortune, heere comes the man, to him Father, for I am a Jewe if I serve the Jewe any longer.

Enter Bassanio *with a follower or two.*

Bass. You may doe so, but let it be so hasted that supper be ready at the farthest by five of the clocke: see these Letters delivered, put the Lyveries to making, and desire *Gratiano* to come anone to my lodging.

Launce. To him Father.

Gob. God blesse your worship.

Bass. Gramercie, wouldst thou ought with me.

Gobbe. Heere's my sonne sir, a poore boy.

Launce. Not a poore boy sir, but the rich Jewes man that would sir as my Father shall specifie.

Gob. He hath a great infection sir, as one would say to serve.

Lau. Indeede the short and the long is, *I* serve the Jewe, & have a desire as my Father shall specifie.

Gob. His Maister and he (saving your worships reverence) are scarce catercosins.

Lau. To be briefe, the very truth is, that the Jewe having done me wrong, dooth cause me as my Father being I hope an old man shall frutifie unto you.

Gob. I have heere a dish of Doves that I would bestow uppon your worship, and my sute is.

Lau. In very briefe, the sute is impertinent to my selfe, as

[55]

your worship shall knowe by this honest old man, and
though I say it, though old man, yet poore man my Father.

Bass. One speake for both, what would you?

Laun. Serve you sir.

Gob. That is the very defect of the matter sir.

Bass. I know thee well, thou hast obtaind thy sute,
Shylocke thy Maister spoke with me this day,
And hath preferd thee, if it be preferment
To leave a rich Jewes service, to become
The follower of so poore a Gentleman.

Clowne. The old proverb is very well parted between my
Maister *Shylocke* and you sir, you have the grace of God sir,
and hee hath enough.

Bass. Thou speakst it well; goe Father with thy Sonne
Take leave of thy old Maister, and enquire
My lodging out, give him a Lyverie
More garded then his fellowes: see it done.

Clowne. Father in, I cannot get a service, no, I have nere a
tong in my head, wel: if any man in Italy have a fayrer table
which dooth offer to sweare upon a booke, I shall have good
fortune; goe too, heere's a simple lyne of life, heeres a small
tryfle of wives, alas, fifteene wives is nothing, a leven
widdoes and nine maydes is a simple comming in for one
man, and then to scape drowning thrice, and to be in perrill
of my life with the edge of a featherbed, heere are simple
scapes: well, if Fortune be a woman she's a good wench for
this gere: Father come, ile take my leave of the Jewe in the
twinkling. *Exit Clowne.*

Bass. I pray thee good *Leonardo* thinke on this,
These things being bought and orderly bestowed
Returne in hast, for I doe feast to night
My best esteemd acquaintance, hie thee goe.

Leon. My best endevours shall be done heerein. *Exit Leonardo.*

Enter Gratiano.

Grati. Where's your Maister.

Leonar. Yonder sir he walkes.

Grati. Signior *Bassanio.*

Bass. Gratiano.

Gra. I have sute to you.

Bass. You have obtaind it.

Gra. You must not deny me, I must goe with you to
Belmont.

Bass. Why then you must but heare thee *Gratiano,*
Thou art to wild, to rude, and bold of voyce,
Parts that become thee happily enough,
And in such eyes as ours appeare not faults
But where thou are not knowne; why there they show
Somthing too liberall, pray thee take paine
To allay with some cold drops of modestie
Thy skipping spirit, least through thy wild behaviour
I be misconstred in the place I goe to,
And loose my hopes.

Gra. Signior *Bassanio,* heare me,
Yf I doe not put on a sober habite,
Talke with respect, and sweare but now and than,
Weare prayer bookes in my pocket, looke demurely,
Nay more, while grace is saying hood mine eyes
Thus with my hat, and sigh and say amen:
Use all the observance of civillity
Like one well studied in a sad ostent
To please his Grandam, never trust me more.

Bass. Well, we shall see your bearing.

Gra. Nay but I barre to night, you shall not gage me
By what we doe to night.

Bass. No that were pitty,
I would intreate you rather to put on
Your boldest sute of mirth, for we have friends
That purpose merriment: but far you well,
I have some busines.

Gra. And I must to *Lorenso* and the rest,
But we will visite you at supper time.　　*Exeunt.*

Enter Jessica *and the Clowne.*

[57]

Jessica. I am sorry thou will leave my Father so,
Our house is hell, and thou a merry devill
Didst rob it of some tast of tediousnes,
But far thee well, there is a ducat for thee,
And *Launcelet*, soone at supper shalt thou see
Lorenso, who is thy new Maisters guest,
Give him this Letter, doe it secretly,
And so farwell: I would not have my Father
See me in talke with thee.

Clowne. Adiew, teares exhibit my tongue, most beautifull
Pagan, most sweete Jewe, if a Christian doe not play the
knave and get thee, I am much deceaved; but adiew, these
foolish drops doe somthing drowne my manly spirit: adiew.

Jessica. Farwell good *Launcelet*.
Alack, what heynous sinne is it in me
To be ashamed to be my Fathers child,
But though I am a daughter to his blood
I am not to his manners: ô *Lorenso*
Yf thou keepe promise I shall end this strife,
Become a Christian and thy loving wife. *Exit.*

Enter Gratiano, Lorenso, Salaryno, and Salanio.

Loren. Nay, we will slinke away in supper time,
Disguise us at my lodging, and returne all in an houre.

Gratia. We have not made good preparation.

Salari. We have not spoke us yet of Torch-bearers,

Solanio. Tis vile unlesse it may be quaintly ordered,
And better in my minde not undertooke.

Loren. Tis now but foure of clocke, we have two houres
To furnish us; friend *Launcelet* whats the newes. *Enter*
                                                    Launcelet

Launcelet. And it shal please you to breake up this, it shal
seeme to signifie.

Loren. I know the hand, in faith tis a faire hand,
And whiter then the paper it writ on
Is the faire hand that writ.

[58]

Gratia. Love, newes in faith.

Launce. By your leave sir.

Loren. Whither goest thou.

Launc. Marry sir to bid my old Maister the *Jewe* to sup to night with my new Maister the Christian.

Loren. Hold heere take this, tell gentle *Jessica*
I will not faile her, speake it privatly,
Goe Gentlemen, will you prepare you for this maske to night,
I am provided of a Torch-bearer.   *Exit Clowne.*

Sal. I marry, ile be gone about it straite.

Sol. And so will *I.*

Loren. Meete me and *Gratiano* at *Gratianos* lodging
Some houre hence.

Sal. Tis good we doe so.   *Exit.*

Gratia. Was not that Letter from faire *Jessica.*

Loren. I must needes tell thee all, she hath directed
How I shall take her from her Fathers house,
What gold and jewels she is furnisht with,
What Pages sute she hath in readines,
Yf ere the Jewe her Father come to heaven,
Yt will be for his gentle daughters sake,
And never dare misfortune crosse her foote,
Unless she doe it under this excuse,
That she is issue to a faithlesse Jewe:
Come goe with me, peruse this as thou goest,
Faire *Jessica* shall be my Torch-bearer.   *Exit.*

Enter Jewe and his man that was the Clowne.

Jewe. Well, thou shalt see, thy eyes shall be thy judge,
The difference of old *Shylocke* and *Bassanio*;
What *Jessica*, thou shalt not gurmandize
As thou hast done with mee: what *Jessica*,
and sleepe, and snore, and rend apparraile out.
Why *Jessica* I say.

Clowne. Why *Jessica.*

Shy. Who bids thee call? I doe not bid thee call.

Clow. Your worship was wont to tell me,

[59]

I could do nothing without bidding.

Enter *Jessica*.

Jessica. Call you? what is your will?

Shy. I am bid forth to supper *Jessica*,
There are my keyes: but wherefore should I goe?
I am not bid for love, they flatter me,
But yet Ile goe in hate, to feede upon
The prodigall Christian. *Jessica* my girle,
looke to my house, *I* am right loth to goe,
There is some ill a bruing towards my rest,
For I did dreame of money baggs to night.

Clowne. I beseech you sir goe, my young Maister
        doth expect your reproch.

Shy. So doe *I* his.

Clowne. And they have conspired together, *I* will not say
you shall see a Maske, but if you doe, then it was not for
nothing that my nose fell a bleeding on black monday last, at
sixe a clocke ith morning, falling out that yeere on ashwensday
was foure yeere in thafternoone.

Shy. What are there maskes? heare you me *Jessica*,
lock up my doores, and when you heare the drumme
and the vile squealing of the wry-neckt Fiffe
clamber not you up to the casements then
Nor thrust your head into the publique streete
To gaze on Christian fooles with varnisht faces:
But stop my houses eares, *I* meane my casements,
let not the sound of shallow fopprie enter
my sober house. By *Jacobs* staffe I sweare
I have no minde of feasting forth to night:
but *J* will goe: goe you before me sirra,
say *I* will come.

Clowne. I will goe before sir.
Mistres looke out at window for all this.
        there will come a Christian by
will be worth a Jewes eye.

Shyl. What sayes that foole of *Hagars* ofspring? ha.

[60]

Jessica. His words were farewell mistris, nothing els.

Shy. The patch is kinde enough, but a huge feeder,
Snaile slow in profit, and he sleepes by day
more then the wild-cat: drones hive not with me,
therefore *I* part with him, and part with him
To one that I would have him helpe to wast
his borrowed purse. Well *Jessica* goe in,
perhaps *I* will returne immediatlie,
do as I bid you, shut dores after you, fast bind, fast find.
a proverbe never stale in thriftie minde.   *Exit.*

Jes. Farewell, and if my fortune be not crost,
I have a Father, you a daughter lost.   *Exit.*

Enter the maskers, *Gratiano* and *Salerino.*

Grat. This is the penthouse under which *Lorenzo*
desired us to make stand.

Sal. His howre is almost past.

Gra. And it is mervaile he out-dwels his howre,
for lovers ever runne before the clocke.

Sal. O tenne times faster *Venus* pidgions flie
to seale loves bonds new made, then they are wont
to keepe obliged faith unforfaited.

Gra. That ever holds: who riseth from a feast
with that keen appetite that he sits downe?
where is the horse that doth untread againe
his tedious measures with the unbated fire
that he did pace them first: all things that are
are with more spirit chased then enjoyd.
How like a younger or a prodigall
the skarfed barke puts from her native bay
hugd and embraced by the strumpet wind,
how like the prodigall doth she returne
with over-wetherd ribbs and ragged sailes
leane, rent, and beggerd by the strumpet wind?

Enter *Lorenzo.*

Sal. Heere comes *Lorenzo*, more of this hereafter.

Lor. Sweet freends, your patience for my long abode
not I but my affaires have made you waite:
when you shall please to play the theeves for wives
Ile watch as long for you then: approch
Here dwels my father Jew. Howe whose within?

Jessica above.

Jess. Who are you? tell me for more certainty,
Albeit Ile sweare that I doe know your tongue.
   Lor. Lorenzo and thy love.
   Jessica. Lorenzo certain, and my love indeed,
for who love I so much? and now who knowes
but you *Lorenzo* whether I am yours?
   Lor. Heaven & thy thoughts are witnes that thou art.
   Jes. Heere catch this casket, it is worth the paines,
I am glad tis night you doe not looke on me,
for I am much ashamde of my exchange:
But love is blinde, and lovers cannot see
The pretty follies that themselves commit,
for if they could, *Cupid* himselfe would blush
to see me thus trans-formed to a boy.
   Lor. Descend, for you must be my torch-bearer.
   Jes. What, must I hold a candle to my shames,
they in themselves goodsooth are too too light.
Why, tis an office of discovery love,
and I should be obscurd.
   Lor. So are you sweet
even in the lovely garnish of a boy, but come at once,
for the close night doth play the runaway,
and we are staid for at *Bassanios* feast.
   Jes. I will make fast the doores & guild my selfe
with some mo ducats, and be with you straight.
   Gra. Now by my hoode a gentle, and no Jew.
   Lor. Beshrow me but I love her hartilie,
For she is wise, if *I* can judge of her,
and faire she is, if that mine eyes be true,
and true she is, as she hath proov'd herselfe:

And therefore like herselfe, wise, faire, and true.
shall she be placed in my constant soule.   Enter *Jessica*.
What, art thou come, on gentleman, away,
our masking mates by this time for us stay.   *Exit*.

Enter *Anthonio*.

An. Whose there?
Gra. Signior *Anthonio*?
Anth. Fie, fie Gratiano, where are all the rest?
Tis nine a clocke, our friends all stay for you,
No maske to night, the wind is come about
Bassanio presently will goe abord,
I have sent twentie out to seeke for you.
Gra. I am glad ont, I desire no more delight
then to be undersaile, and gone to night.   *Exeunt*.

Enter *Portia* with *Morrocho* and both
theyr traines.

Por. Goe, draw aside the curtaines and discover
the severall caskets to this noble Prince:
Now make your choyse.
Mor. This first of gold, who this inscription beares,
Who chooseth me, shall gaine what many men desire.
The second silver, which this promise carries,
Who chooseth me, shall get as much as he deserves.
This third, dull lead, with warning all as blunt,
Who chooseth me, must give and hazard all he hath.
How shall I know if I doe choose the right?
Por. The one of them containes my picture Prince,
if you choose that, then I am yours withall.
Mor. Some God direct my judgement, let me see,
I will survay th'inscriptions, back againe,
What saies this leaden casket?
Who chooseth me, must give and hazard all he hath,
Must give, for what? for lead, hazard for lead?
This casket threatens men that hazard all
doe it in hope of faire advantages:

A golden minde stoopes not to showes of drosse,
Ile then nor give nor hazard ought for lead.
What sayes the silver with her virgin hue?
Who chooseth me, shal get as much as he deserves.
As much as he deserves, pause there *Morocho*,
and weigh thy valew with an even hand,
If thou beest rated by thy estimation
thou doost deserve enough, and yet enough
May not extend so farre as to the Ladie:
And yet to be afeard of my deserving
were but a weake disabling of my selfe.
As much as *I* deserve, why thats the Ladie.
I doe in birth deserve her, and in fortunes,
in graces, and in qualities of breeding:
but more then these, in love *I* doe deserve,
what if *I* straid no farther, but chose heere?
Lets see once more this saying grav'd in gold:
Who chooseth me shall gaine what many men desire:
Why thats the Ladie, all the world desires her.
From the foure corners of the earth they come
to kisse this shrine, this mortall breathing Saint.
The Hircanion deserts, and the vastie wildes
Of wide Arabia are as throughfares now
for Princes to come view faire *Portia*.
The waterie Kingdome, whose ambitious head
Spets in the face of heaven, is no barre
To stop the forraine spirits, but they come
as ore a brooke to see faire *Portia*.
One of these three containes her heavenly picture.
*I*st like that leade containes her, twere damnation
to thinke so base a thought, it were too grosse
to ribb her serecloth in the obscure grave,
Or shall I think in silver shees immurd
beeing tenne times undervalewed to tride gold,
O sinful thought, never so rich a *Jem*
was set in worse then gold. They have in England
A coyne that beares the figure of an Angell

[64]

stampt in gold, but thats insculpt upon:
But heere an Angell in a golden bed
lies all within. Deliver me the key:
heere doe I choose, and thrive I as I may.

Por. There take it Prince, and if my forme lie there
then I am yours?

Mor. O hell! what have wee heare, a carrion death,
within whose emptie eye there is a written scroule,
Ile reade the writing.

> *All that glisters is not gold,*
> *Often have you heard that told,*
> *Many a man his life hath sold*
> *But my outside to behold,*
> *Guilded timber doe wormes infold:*
> *Had you beene as wise as bold,*
> *Young in limbs, in judgement old,*
> *Your aunswere had not beene inscrold,*
> *Fareyouwell, your sute is cold.*

Mor. Cold indeede and labour lost,
Then farewell heate, and welcome frost:
Portia adiew, I have too greev'd a hart
To take a tedious leave: thus loosers part.   *Exit.*

Por. A gentle riddance, draw the curtaines, go,
Let all of his complexion choose me so.   *Exeunt.*

Enter *Salarino* and *Solanio.*

Sal. Why man I saw *Bassanio* under sayle,
with him is *Gratiano* gone along;
and in theyr ship I am sure *Lorenzo* is not.

Sola. The villaine Jew with outcries raisd the Duke,
who went with him to search *Bassanios* ship.

Sal. He came too late, the ship was undersaile,
But there the Duke was given to understand
that in a Gondylo were seene together
Lorenzo and his amorous *Jessica.*
Besides, *Anthonio* certified the Duke
they were not with *Bassanio* in his ship.

Sol. I never heard a passion so confusd,
So strange, outragious, and so variable
as the dogge Jew did utter in the streets,
My daughter, ô my ducats, ô my daughter,
Fled with a Christian, ô my Christian ducats.
Justice, the law, my ducats, and my daughter,
A sealed bag, two sealed bags of ducats
of double ducats, stolne from me by my daughter,
and Jewels, two stones, two rich and precious stones,
Stolne by my daughter: justice, find the girle,
shee hath the stones upon her, and the ducats.

Sal. Why all the boyes in Venice follow him,
crying his stones, his daughter, and his ducats.

Sola. Let good *Anthonio* looke he keepe his day
or he shall pay for this.

Sal. Marry well remembred.
I reasond with a Frenchman yesterday,
who told me, in the narrow seas that part
the French and English, there miscaried
a vessell of our country richly fraught:
I thought upon *Anthonio* when he told me,
and wisht in silence that it were not his.

Sol. You were best to tell *Anthonio* what you heare;
Yet doe not suddainely, for it may greeve him.

Sal. A kinder gentleman treades not the earth,
I saw *Bassanio* and *Anthonio* part,
Bassanio told him he would make some speede
of his returne: he aunswered, doe not so,
slumber not busines for my sake *Bassanio*,
but stay the very riping of the time,
and for the Jewes bond which he hath of me
let it not enter in your minde of love:
be merry, and imploy your cheefest thoughts
to courtship, and such fair ostents of love
as shall conveniently become you there,
And even there his eye being big with teares,
turning his face, he put his hand behind him,

and with affection wondrous sencible
He wrung *Bassanios*, and so they parted.
   Sol. I thinke hee onely loves the world for him,
I pray thee let us goe and finde him out
and quicken his embraced heavines
with some delight or other.
   Sal. Doe we so.   *Exeunt.*

Enter *Nerrissa* and a Serviture.

   Ner. Quick, quick I pray thee, draw the curtain strait,
The Prince of Arragon hath tane his oath,
and comes to his election presently.

Enter *Arrogon*, his trayne, and *Portia*.

   Por. Behold, there stand the caskets noble Prince,
yf you choose that wherein I am containd
straight shall our nuptiall rights be solemniz'd:
but if you faile, without more speech my Lord
you must be gone from hence immediatly.
   Arra. I am enjoynd by oath to observe three things,
First, never to unfold to any one
which casket twas I chose; next, if I faile
of the right casket, never in my life
to wooe a maide in way of marriage:
lastly, if I doe faile in fortune of my choyse,
immediatly to leave you, and be gone.
   Por. To these injunctions every one doth sweare
that comes to hazard for my worthlesse selfe.
   Arr. And so have I addrest me, fortune now
To my harts hope: gold, silver, and base lead.
Who chooseth me, must give and hazard all he hath.
You shall looke fairer ere I give or hazard.
What saies the golden chest, ha, let me see,
Who chooseth me, shall gaine what many men desire,
What many men desire, that many may be meant
by the foole multitude that choose by show,
not learning more then the fond eye doth teach,

which pries not to thinteriour, but like the Martlet
Builds in the weather on the outward wall,
Even in the force and rode of casualty.
I will not choose what many men desire,
Because I will not jumpe with common spirits,
And ranke me with the barbarous multitudes.
Why then to thee thou silver treasure house,
Tell me once more what title thou doost beare;
Who chooseth me shall get as much as he deserves,
And well sayde to; for who shall goe about
To cosen Fortune, and be honourable
without the stampe of merrit, let none presume
To weare an undeserved dignity:
O that estates, degrees, and offices,
were not deriv'd corruptly, and that cleare honour
were purchast by the merit of the wearer,
How many then should cover that stand bare?
How many be commaunded that commaund?
How much low peasantry would then be gleaned
From the true seede of honour? and how much honour
Pickt from the chaft and ruin of the times,
To be new varnisht; well but to my choise.
Who chooseth me shall get as much as he deserves,
I will assume desert; give me a key for this,
And instantly unlocke my fortunes heere.

   Portia. Too long a pause for that which you finde there.

   Arrag. What's heere, the pourtrait of a blinking idiot
Presenting me a shedule, I will read it:
How much unlike art thou to *Portia*?
How much unlike my hopes and my deservings.
Who chooseth me, shall have as much as he deserves?
Did I deserve no more then a fooles head,
Is that my prize, are my deserts no better?

   Portia. To offend and judge are distinct offices,
And of opposed natures.

   Arrag. What is heere?

      The fier seaven times tried this,

[68]

> *Seaven times tried that judement is,*
> *That did never choose amis,*
> *Some there be that shadowes kis.*
> *Such have but a shadowes blis:*
> *There be fooles alive Iwis*
> *Silverd o're, and so was this.*
> *Take what wife you will to bed,*
> *I will ever be your head:*
> *So be gone, you are sped.*

Arrag. Still more foole I shall appeare
By the time I linger heere,
With one fooles head *I* came to woo,
But I goe away with two.
Sweet adiew, ile keepe my oath,
Paciently to beare my wroath.

    Portia. Thus hath the candle singd the moath:
O these deliberate fooles when they doe choose,
They have the wisedome by their wit to loose.

    Nerriss. The aunccient saying is no herisie,
Hanging and wiving goes by destinie.

    Portia. Come draw the curtaine *Nerrissa.*

Enter Messenger.

    Mess. Where is my Lady.

    Portia. Heere, what would my Lord?

    Mess. Madame, there is a-lighted at your gate
A young Venetian, one that comes before
To signifie th'approching of his Lord,
From whom he bringeth sensible regreets;
To wit, (besides commends and curtious breath)
Gifts of rich valiew; yet I have not seene
So likely an Embassador of love,
A day in Aprill never came so sweete
To show how costly Sommer was at hand,
As this fore-spurrer comes before his Lord.

    Portia. No more I pray thee, *I* am halfe-a-feard
That wilt say anone he is some kin to thee,

[69]

Thou spendst such high day wit in praysing him:
Come come *Nerryssa*, for I long to see
Quick *Cupids* Post that comes so mannerly.

    Nerryss. Bassanio Lord, love if thy will it be.   *Exeunt.*

    Solanio and Salarino.

    Solanio. Now what newes on the Ryalto?

    Salari. Why yet it lives there uncheckt, that *Anthonio* hath a ship of rich lading wrackt on the narrow Seas; the Goodwins I thinke they call the place, a very dangerous flat, and fatall, where the carcasses of many a tall ship lie buried, as they say, if my gossip report be an honest woman of her word.

    Solanio. I would she were as lying a gossip in that, as ever knapt Ginger, or made her neighbours beleeve she wept for the death of a third husband: but it is true, without any slips of prolixity, or crossing the plaine high way of talke, that the good *Anthonio*, the honest *Anthonio*; ô that *I* had a tytle good enough to keepe his name company.

    Salari. Come, the full stop.

    Solanio. Ha, what sayest thou, why the end is, he hath lost a ship.

    Salari. I would it might prove the end of his losses.

    Solanio. Let me say amen betimes, least the devil crosse my praier, for heere he comes in the likenes of a Jewe. How now *Shylocke*, what newes among the Merchants?   *Enter Shylocke.*

    Shy. You knew, none so well, none so well as you, of my daughters flight.

    Salari. Thats certaine, *I* for my part knew the Taylor that made the wings she flew withall.

    Solan. And *Shylocke* for his own part knew the bird was flidge, and then it is the complexion of them all to leave the dam.

    Shy. She is damnd for it.

    Salari. Thats certaine, if the devill may be her Judge.

    Shy. My owne flesh and blood to rebell.

    Sola. Out upon it old carrion, rebels it at these yeeres.

    Shy. I say my daughter is my flesh and my blood.

Salari. There is more difference betweene thy flesh and hers, then between *Jet* and *Ivorie*, more betweene your bloods, then there is betweene red wine and rennish: but tell us, doe you heare whether *Anthonio* have had any losse at sea or no?

Shy. There I have another bad match, a bankrout, a prodigall, who dare scarce shewe his head on the Ryalto, a begger that was usd to come so smug upon the Mart: let him looke to his bond, he was wont to call me usurer, let him looke to his bond, hee was wont to lende money for a Christian cursie, let him looke to his bond.

Salari. Why I am sure if he forfaite, thou wilt not take his flesh, what's that good for?

Shyl. To baite fish with all, if it will feede nothing else, it will feede my revenge; hee hath disgrac'd me, and hindred me halfe a million, laught at my losses, mockt at my gaines, scorned my Nation, thwarted my bargaines, cooled my friends, heated mine enemies, and whats his reason, I am a Jewe: Hath not a Jewe eyes, hath not a Jewe hands, organs, dementions, sences, affections, passions, fed with the same foode, hurt with the same weapons, subject to the same diseases, healed by the same meanes, warmed and cooled by the same Winter and Sommer as a Christian is: if you pricke us doe we not bleede, if you tickle us doe wee not laugh, if you poyson us doe wee not die, and if you wrong us shall wee not revenge, if we are like you in the rest, we will resemble you in that. If a Jewe wrong a Christian, what is his humillity, revenge? If a Christian wrong a Jewe, what should his sufferance be by Christian example, why revenge? The villanie you teach me I will execute, and it shall goe hard but I will better the instruction.

Enter a man from Anthonio.

Gentlemen, my maister Anthonio is at his house, and desires to speake with you both.

Saleri. We have beene up and downe to seeke him.

Enter Tuball.

[71]

Solanio. Heere comes another of the Tribe, a third cannot bee matcht, unlesse the devill himselfe turne Jewe. *Exeunt*

Gentlemen.

Enter Tuball.

Shy. How now *Tuball*, what newes from Genowa, hast thou found my daughter?

Tuball. I often came where I did heare of her, but cannot finde her.

Shylocke. Why there, there, there, there, a diamond gone cost me two thousand ducats in Franckford, the curse never fell upon our Nation till now, I never felt it till nowe, two thousand ducats in that, & other precious precious jewels; I would my daughter were dead at my foote, and the jewels in her eare: would she were hearst at my foote, and the ducats in her coffin: no newes of them, why so? and I know not whats spent in the search: why thou losse upon losse, the theefe gone with so much, and so much to finde the theefe, and no satisfaction, no revenge, nor no ill luck stirring but what lights a my shoulders, no sighs but a my breathing, no teares but a my shedding.

Tuball. Yes, other men have ill lucke to, *Anthonio* as I heard in Genowa?

Shy. What, what, what, ill lucke, ill lucke.

Tuball. Hath an Argosie cast away comming from Tripolis.

Shy. I thank God, *I* thank God, is it true, is it true.

Tuball. I spoke with some of the Saylers that escaped the wrack.

Shy. I thank thee good *Tuball*, good newes, good newes: ha ha, heere in Genowa.

Tuball. Your daughter spent in Genowa, as I heard, one night fourescore ducats.

Shy. Thou stickst a dagger in me, I shall never see my gold againe, foure score ducats at a sitting, foure score ducats.

Tuball. There came divers of *Anthonios* creditors in my company to Venice, that sweare, he cannot choose but breake.

Shy. I am very glad of it, ile plague him, ile torture him, *I* am glad of it.

Tuball. One of them shewed mee a ring that hee had of your daughter for a Monky.

Shy. Out upon her, thou torturest mee *Tuball*, it was my Turkies, I had it of *Leah* when I was a Batcheler: I would not have given it for a Wildernes of Monkies.

Tuball. But *Anthonio* is certainly undone.

Shy. Nay, that's true, that's very true, goe *Tuball* fee me an Officer, bespeake him a fortnight before, I will have the hart of him if he forfeite, for were he out of Venice I can make what merchandize I will: goe *Tuball*, and meete me at our Sinagogue, goe good *Tuball*, at our Sinagogue *Tuball*. *Exeunt.*

Enter Bassanio, Portia, Gratiano, and all their traynes.

Portia. I pray you tarry, pause a day or two
Before you hazard, for in choosing wrong
I loose your companie; therefore forbeare a while,
Theres something tells me (but it is not love)
I would not loose you, and you know your selfe,
Hate counsailes not in such a quallity;
But least you should not understand me well,
And yet a mayden hath no tongue, but thought,
I would detaine you heere some moneth or two
before you venture for me. I could teach you
how to choose right, but then I am forsworne,
So will *I* never be, so may you misse me,
But if you doe, youle make me wish a sinne,
That *I* had beene forsworne: Beshrow your eyes,
They have ore-lookt me and devided me,
One halfe of me is yours, the other halfe yours,
Mine owne I would say: but if mine then yours,
And so all yours; ô these naughty times
puts barres betweene the owners and their rights.
And so though yours, not yours, (prove it so)

[73]

Let Fortune goe to hell for it, not I.
I speake too long, but tis to peize the time,
To ech it, and to draw it out in length,
To stay you from election.

    Bass. Let me choose,
For as *I* am, *I* live upon the racke.

    Por. Upon the racke *Bassanio*, then confesse
what treason there is mingled with your love.

    Bass. None but that ugly treason of mistrust,
which makes me feare th'injoying of my Love,
There may as well be amity and life
Tweene snow and fire, as treason and my love.

    Por. I but I feare you speake upon the racke
where men enforced doe speake any thing.

    Bass. Promise me life, and ile confesse the truth.

    Portia. Well then, confesse and live.

    Bass. Confesse and love
had beene the very sum of my confession:
O happy torment, when my torturer
doth teach me aunsweres for deliverance:
But let me to my fortune and the caskets.

    Portia. Away then, I am lockt in one of them,
If you doe love me, you will finde me out.
Nerryssa and the rest, stand all aloofe,
Let musique sound while he doth make his choyse,
Then if he loose he makes a Swan-like end,
Fading in musique. That the comparison
may stand more proper, my eye shall be the streame
and watry death-bed for him: he may win,
And what is musique than? Than musique is
even as the flourish, when true subjects bowe
to a new crowned Monarch: Such it is,
As are those dulcet sounds in breake of day,
That creepe into the dreaming bride-groomes eare,
And summon him to marriage. Now he goes
with no lesse presence, but with much more love
Then young Alcides, when he did redeeme

The virgine tribute, payed by howling Troy
To the Sea-monster: I stand for sacrifice,
The rest aloofe are the Dardanian wives:
With bleared visages come forth to view
The issue of th'exploit: Goe Hercules,
Live thou, I live with much much more dismay,
I view the fight, then thou that mak'st the fray.

*A Song the whilst Bassanio comments on the caskets
to himselfe.*

Tell me where is fancie bred,
Or in the hart, or in the head,
How begot, how nourished?   *Replie, replie.*
It is engendred in the eye,
With gazing fed, and Fancie dies:
In the cradle where it lies
Let us all ring Fancies knell.
Ile begin it.
Ding, dong, bell.
  All. *Ding, dong, bell.*
  Bass. So may the outward showes be least themselves,
The world is still deceav'd with ornament
In Law, what plea so tainted and corrupt,
But being season'd with a gracious voyce,
Obscures the show of evill. In religion
What damned error but some sober brow
will blesse it, and approve it with a text,
Hiding the grosnes with faire ornament:
There is no voyce so simple, but assumes
Some marke of vertue on his outward parts;
How many cowards whose harts are all as false
As stayers of sand, weare yet upon their chins
The beards of *Hercules* and frowning *Mars*,
who inward searcht, have lyvers white as milke,
And these assume but valours excrement
To render them redoubted. Looke on beauty,
And you shall see tis purchast by the weight,

[75]

which therein works a miracle in nature,
Making them lightest that weare most of it:
So are those crisped snaky golden locks
which maketh such wanton gambols with the wind
Upon supposed fairnes, often knowne
To be the dowry of a second head,
The scull that bred them in the Sepulcher.
Thus ornament is but the guiled shore
To a most dangerous sea: the beautious scarfe
vailing an Indian beauty; In a word,
The seeming truth which cunning times put on
To intrap the wisest. Therefore then thou gaudy gold,
Hard food for *Midas*, I will none of thee,
Nor none of thee thou pale and common drudge
tweene man and man: but thou, thou meager lead
Which rather threatenst then dost promise ought,
Thy palenes moves me more then eloquence,
and heere choose I, joy be the consequence.

Por. How all the other passions fleet to ayre,
As doubtfull thoughts, and rash imbrac'd despaire:
And shyddring feare, and greene-eyed jealousie.
O love be moderate, allay thy extasie,
In measure raine thy joy, scant this excesse,
I feele too much thy blessing, make it lesse
for feare *I* surfeit.

Bas. What finde I heere?
Faire *Portias* counterfeit. What demy God
hath come so neere creation? move these eyes?
Or whither riding on the balls of mine
seeme they in motion? Heere are severd lips
parted with suger breath, so sweet a barre
should sunder such sweet friends: heere in her haires
the Paynter playes the Spyder, and hath woven
a golden mesh tyntrap the harts of men
faster then gnats in cobwebs, but her eyes
how could he see to doe them? having made one,
me thinkes it should have power to steale both his

[76]

and leave it selfe unfurnisht: Yet looke how farre
the substance of my praise doth wrong this shadow
in underprysing it, so farre this shadow
doth limpe behind the substance. Heeres the scroule,
the continent and summarie of my fortune.

> *You that choose not by the view*
> *Chaunce as faire, and choose as true:*
> *Since this fortune falls to you,*
> *Be content, and seeke no new.*
> *If you be well pleasd with this,*
> *And hold your fortune for your blisse,*
> *Turne you where your Lady is,*
> *And claime her with a loving kis.*

A gentle scroule: Faire Lady, by your leave,
I come by note to give, and to receave,
Like one of two contending in a prize
That thinks he hath done well in people's eyes:
Hearing applause and universall shoute,
Giddy in spirit, still gazing in a doubt
whether those peales of praise be his or no,
So thrice faire Lady stand I even so,
As doubtfull whether what I see be true,
Until confirmd, signd, ratified by you.

Por. You see me Lord *Bassanio* where I stand,
such as I am; though for my selfe alone
I would not be ambitious in my wish
to wish my self much better, yet for you,
I would be trebled twentie times my selfe,
a thousand times more faire, tenne thousand times
more rich, that onely to stand high in your account,
I might in vertues, beauties, livings, friends
exceede account: but the full summe of me
is sume of something: which to terme in grosse
is an unlessond girle, unschoold, unpractized,
happy in this, she is not yet so old
but she may learne: happier then this,
shee is not bred so dull but she can learne;

[77]

happiest of all, is that her gentle spirit
commits it selfe to yours to be directed,
as from her Lord, her governour, her King.
My selfe, and what is mine, to you and yours
is now converted. But now I was the Lord
of this faire mansion, maister of my servants,
Queene ore my selfe: and even now, but now,
this house, these servaunts, and this same my selfe
are yours, my Lords, I give them with this ring,
which when you part from, loose, or give away,
let it presage the ruine of your love,
and be my vantage to exclaime on you.

    Bass. Maddam, you have bereft me of all words,
onely my blood speakes to you in my vaines,
and there is such confusion in my powers,
as after some oration fairely spoke
by a beloved Prince, there doth appeare
among the buzzing pleased multitude.
Where every somthing beeing blent together,
turnes to a wild of nothing, save of joy
exprest, and not exprest: but when this ring
parts from this finger, then parts life from hence,
ô then be bold to say *Bassanios* dead.

    Ner. My Lord and Lady, it is now our time
that have stoode by and seene our wishes prosper,
to cry good joy, good joy my Lord and Lady.

    Gra. My Lord *Bassanio*, and my gentle Lady,
I wish you all the joy that you can wish:
For *I* am sure you can wish none from me:
and when your honours meane to solemnize
the bargaine of your fayth: I doe beseech you
even at that time I may be married to.

    Bass. With all my hart, so thou canst get a wife.

    Gra. I thanke your Lordship, you have got me one.
My eyes my Lord can looke as swift as yours:
you saw the mistres, I beheld the mayd:
You lov'd, *I* lov'd for intermission,

No more pertaines to me my lord then you;
your fortune stood upon the caskets there,
and so did mine to as the matter falls:
for wooing heere untill *I* swet againe,
and swearing till my very rough was dry
with oathes of love, at last, if promise last
I got a promise of this faire one heere
to have her love: provided that your fortune
atchiv'd her mistres.

   Por. Is this true *Nerrissa*?

   Ner. Maddam it is, so you stand pleasd withall.

   Bass. And doe you *Gratiano* meane good fayth?

   Gra. Yes faith my Lord.

   Bass. Our feast shalbe much honored in your mariage.

   Gra. Wele play with them the first boy for a thousand
ducats.

   Ner. What and stake down?

   Gra. No, we shall nere win at that sport and stake downe.
But who comes heere? *Lorenzo* and his infidell?
what, and my old Venecian friend *Salerio*?

      Enter *Lorenzo*, *Jessica*, and *Salerio* a messenger
                from Venice.

   Bassa. Lorenzo and *Salerio*, welcome hether,
if that the youth of my newe intrest heere
have power to bid you welcome: by your leave
I bid my very friends and countrymen
sweet *Portia* welcome.

   Por. So doe I my Lord, they are intirely welcome.

   Lor. I thanke your honour, for my part my Lord
my purpose was not to have seene you heere,
but meeting with *Salerio* by the way
he did intreate me past all saying nay
to come with him along.

   Sal. I did my Lord,
and I have reason for it, Signior *Anthonio*
commends him to you.

[79]

Bass. Ere I ope his Letter
I pray you tell me how my good friend doth.

   Sal. Not sicke my Lord, unlesse it be in mind,
nor well, unlesse in mind: his letter there
will show you his estate.   *open the letter.*

   Gra. *Nerrissa*, cheere yond stranger, bid her welcom.
Your hand *Salerio*, what's the newes from Venice?
How doth that royall Merchant good *Anthonio*?
I know he will be glad of our successe,
We are the *Jasons*, we have won the fleece.

   Sal. I would you had won the fleece that he hath lost.

   Por. There are some shrowd contents in yond same paper
That steales the colour from *Bassanios* cheeke,
Some deere friend dead, else nothing in the world
could turne so much the constitution
of any constant man: what worse and worse?
With leave *Bassanio* I am halfe your selfe,
and I must freely have the halfe of any thing
that this same paper brings you.

   Bass. O sweete *Portia*,
heere are a few of the unpleasant'st words
that ever blotted paper. Gentle Lady
when I did first impart my love to you,
I freely told you all the wealth I had
ranne in my vaines, I was a gentleman,
and then *I* told you true: and yet deere Lady
rating my selfe at nothing, you shall see
how much *I* was a Braggart, when I told you
my state was nothing. I should then have told you
that *I* was worse then nothing; for indeede
I have ingag'd my selfe to a deere friend,
ingag'd my friend to his meere enemie
to feede my meanes. Heere is a letter Lady,
the paper as the body of my friend,
and every word in it a gaping wound
issuing life blood. But is it true *Salerio*
hath all his ventures faild, what not one hit,

from Tripolis, from Mexico and England,
from Lisbon, Barbary, and India,
and not one vessell scape the dreadfull touch
of Merchant-marring rocks?

    Sal. Not one my Lord.
Besides, it should appeare, that if he had
the present money to discharge the Jew,
hee would not take it: never did *I* know
a creature that did beare the shape of man
so keene and greedie to confound a man.
He plyes the Duke at morning and at night,
and doth impeach the freedome of the state
if they deny him justice. Twentie Merchants,
the Duke himselfe, and the Magnificoes
of greatest port have all perswaded with him,
but none can drive him from the envious plea
of forfaiture, of justice, and his bond.

    Jessi. When I was with him, I have heard him sweare
to *Tuball* and to *Chus,* his country-men,
that he would rather have *Anthonios* flesh,
then twentie times the value of the summe
that he did owe him: and I know my lord,
if law, authoritie, and power denie not,
it will goe hard with poore *Anthonio.*

    Por. Is it your deere friend that is thus in trouble?

    Bass. The deerest friend to me, the kindest man,
the best conditiond and unwearied spirit
in dooing curtesies: and one in whom
the auncient Romaine honour more appeares
then any that drawes breath in *Italie.*

    Por. What summe owes he the Jew?

    Bass. For me three thousand ducats.

    Por. What no more, pay him six thousand, & deface the bond:
double six thousand, and then treble that,
before a friend of this discription
shall lose a haire through *Bassanios* fault.
First goe with me to Church, and call me wife,

and then away to Venice to your friend:
for never shall you lie by *Portias* side
with an unquiet soule. You shall have gold
to pay the petty debt twenty times over.
When it is payd, bring your true friend along,
my mayd *Nerrissa*, and my selfe meane time
will live as maydes and widdowes; come away,
for you shall hence upon your wedding day:
bid your freends welcome, show a merry cheere,
since you are deere bought, I will love you deere.
But let me heare the letter of your friend.

 Sweet Bassanio, *my ships have all miscaried, my Creditors growe cruell, my estate is very low, my bond to the Jewe is forfaite, and since in paying it, it is impossible I should live, all debts are cleerd betweene you and I if I might but see you at my death: notwithstanding, use your pleasure, if your love do not perswade you to come, let not my letter.*

 Por. O love! dispatch all busines and be gone.
 Bass. Since *I* have your good leave to goe away,
I will make hast; but till I come againe,
no bed shall ere be guiltie of my stay,
nor rest be interposer twixt us twaine.

Exeunt.

Enter the *Jew*, and *Salerio*, and *Anthonio*,
and the Jaylor.

 Jew. Jaylor, looke to him, tell not me of mercie,
this is the foole that lent out money gratis.
Jaylor, looke to him.
 Ant. Heare me yet good *Shylock*.
 Jew. Ile have my bond, speake not against my bond,
I have sworne an oath, that I will have my bond:
thou call'dst me dogge before thou hadst a cause,
but since I am a dog, beware my phanges,
the Duke shall graunt me justice, *I* do wonder
thou naughtie *Jaylor* that thou art so fond
to come abroade with him at his request.

An. I pray thee heare me speake.

Jew. Ile have my bond, I will not heare thee speake,
Ile have my bond, and therefore speake no more.
Ile not be made a soft and dull eyde foole,
to shake the head, relent, and sigh, and yeeld
to christian intercessers: follow not,
Ile have no speaking, *I* will have my bond.

                                         Exit Jew.

   Sol. It is the most impenitrable curre
       that ever kept with men.

   An. Let him alone,
Ile follow him no more with bootlesse prayers.
hee seekes my life, his reason well *I* know;
I oft deliverd from his forfeytures
many that have at times made mone to me,
therefore he hates me.

   Sal. I am sure the Duke will never grant
       this forfaiture to hold.

   An. The Duke cannot denie the course of law:
for the commoditie that strangers have
with us in Venice, if it be denyed,
will much impeach the justice of the state,
since that the trade and profit of the citty
consisteth of all Nations. Therefore goe,
these griefes and losses have so bated me
that *I* shall hardly spare a pound of flesh
to morrow, to my bloody Creditor.
Well Jaylor, on pray God *Bassanio* come
to see me pay his debt, and then *I* care not. *Exeunt*

         Enter *Portia, Nerrissa, Lorenzo, Jessica,* and a
                        man of *Portias.*

   Lor. Maddam, although I speake it in your presence,
you have a noble and a true conceite
of god-like amitie, which appeares most strongly
in bearing thus the absence of your Lord.
But if you knew to whom you show this honour,

how true a gentleman you send releefe,
how deere a lover of my Lord your husband,
I know you would be prouder of the worke
then customarie bountie can enforce you.

   Por. I never did repent for dooing good,
nor shall not now: for in companions
that doe converse and wast the time together,
whose soules doe beare an egall yoke of love,
there must be needes a like proportion
of lyniaments, of manners, and of spirit;
which makes me thinke that this *Anthonio*
beeing the bosome lover of my Lord,
must needes be like my Lord. If it be so,
How little is the cost I have bestowed
in purchasing the semblance of my soule;
From out the state of hellish cruelty,
This comes too neere the praising of my selfe,
Therefore no more of it: heere other things
Lorenso I commit unto your hands,
The husbandry and mannage of my house,
Untill my Lords return: for mine owne part
I have toward heaven breath'd a secret vowe,
To live in prayer and contemplation,
Onely attended by *Nerrissa* heere,
Untill her husband and my Lords returne,
There is a Monastry two miles off
And there we will abide. I doe desire you
not to denie this imposition,
the which my love and some necessity
now layes upon you.

   Loren. Madame, with all my hart,
I shall obey you in all faire commaunds.

   Por. My people doe already know my mind,
And will acknowledge you and *Jessica*
in place of Lord *Bassanio* and my selfe.
So far you well till we shall meete againe.

   Lor. Faire thoughts and happy houres attend on you.

Jessi. I wish your Ladiship all harts content.

Por. I thank you for your wish, and am well pleasd
to wish it back on you: far you well *Jessica.*　　　　*Exeunt.*
Now *Balthaser,* as I have ever found thee honest true,
So let me find thee still: take this same letter,
and use thou all th'indevour of a man,
In speede to Mantua, see thou render this
into my cosin hands Doctor *Belario,*
And looke what notes and garments he doth give thee,
bring them *I* pray thee with imagin'd speede
unto the Tranect, to the common Ferrie
which trades to Venice; wast no time in words
but get thee gone, I shall be there before thee.

Baltha. Madam, I goe with all convenient speede.

Portia. Come on *Nerrissa,* I have worke in hand
That you yet know not of; weele see our husbands
before they thinke of us?

Nerrissa. Shall they see us?

Portia. They shall *Nerrissa:* but in such a habite,
that they shall thinke we are accomplished
with that we lacke; Ile hold thee any wager
when we are both accoutered like young men,
ile prove the prettier fellow of the two,
and weare my dagger with the braver grace,
and speake betweene the change of man and boy,
with a reede voyce, and turne two minsing steps
into a manly stride; and speake of frayes
like a fine bragging youth: and tell quaint lyes
how honorable Ladies sought my love,
which I denying, they fell sicke and dyed.
I could not doe withall: then ile repent,
and wish for all that, that I had not killd them;
And twentie of these punie lies ile tell,
that men shall sweare I have discontinued schoole
above a twelve-moneth: I have within my minde
a thousand raw tricks of these bragging Jacks,
which I will practise.

[85]

Nerriss. Why, shall we turne to men?

Portia. Fie, what a question's that,
if thou were nere a lewd interpreter:
But come, ile tell thee all my whole device
when I am in my coach, which stayes for us
at the Parke gate; and therefore hast away,
for we must measure twenty miles to day.   *Exeunt.*

Enter Clowne and Jessica.

Clowne. Yes truly, for looke you, the sinnes of the Father
are to be laid upon the children, therefore I promise you, I
feare you, I was alwaies plaine with you, and so now I speake
my agitation of the matter: therefore be a good chere, for
truly I thinke you are damnd, there is but one hope in it that
can doe you any good, and that is but a kinde of bastard hope
neither.

Jessica. And what hope is that I pray thee?

Clowne. Marry you may partly hope that your Father got
you not, that you are not the Jewes daughter.

Jessica. That were a kind of bastard hope in deede, so the
sinnes of my mother should be visited upon me.

Clowne. Truly then I feare you are damnd both by father
and mother: thus when I shun *Scilla* your father, I fall into
Caribdis your mother; well, you are gone both wayes.

Jessica. I shall be sav'd by my husband, he hath made me a
Christian?

Clowne. Truly the more to blame he, we were Christians
enow before, in as many as could well live one by another:
this making of Christians will raise the price of Hogs, if we
grow all to be pork eaters, we shall not shortly have a rasher
on the coles for mony.

Enter Lorenzo.

Jessi. Ile tell my husband *Launcelet* what you say, here he
come?

Loren. I shall grow jealous of you shortly *Launcelet*, if you
thus get my wife into corners?

Jessica. Nay, you neede not feare us *Lorenzo*, *Launcelet* and

[86]

I are out, he tells me flatly there's no mercy for mee in heaven, because I am a Jewes daughter: and he sayes you are no good member of the common-wealth, for in converting Jewes to Christians, you raise the price of porke.

Loren. I shall aunswere that better to the common-wealth than you can the getting up of the Negroes belly: the Moore is with child by you *Launcelet*?

Clowne. It is much that the Moore should be more then reason: but if she be lesse then an honest woman, she is indeede more then I took her for.

Loren. How every foole can play upon the word, I thinke the best grace of wit will shortly turne into silence, and discourse grow commendable in none onely but Parrats: goe in sirra, bid them prepare for dinner?

Clowne. That is done sir, they have all stomacks?

Loren. Goodly Lord what a wit snapper are you, than bid them prepare dinner?

Clowne. That is done to sir, onely cover is the word.

Loren. Will you cover than sir?

Clowne. Not so sir neither, I know my duty.

Loren. Yet more quarrelling with occasion, wilt thou shewe the whole wealth of thy wit in an instant; I pray thee understand a plaine man in his plaine meaning: goe to thy fellowes, bid them cover the table, serve in the meate, and we will come in to dinner.

Clowne. For the table sir, it shall be serv'd in, for the meate sir, it shall be coverd, for your comming in to dinner sir, why let it be as humors and conceites shall governe. *Exit Clowne.*

Loren. O deare discretion, how his words are suted,
The foole hath planted in his memorie
an Armie of good words, and I doe know
a many fooles that stand in better place,
garnisht like him, that for a tricksie word
defie the matter: how cherst thou *Jessica*,
And now good sweet say thy opinion,
How doost thou like the Lord *Bassanio's* wife?

Jessi. Past all expressing, it is very meete
the Lord *Bassanio* live an upright life
For having such a blessing in his Lady,
he findes the joyes of heaven heere on earth,
And if on earth he doe not meane it, it
in reason he should never come to heaven?
Why, if two Gods should play some heavenly match,
and on the wager lay two earthly women,
And *Portia* one: there must be somthing else
paund with the other, for the poore rude world
hath not her fellow.

Loren. Even such a husband
hast thou of me, as she is for wife.

Jessi. Nay, but aske my opinion to of that?

Loren. I will anone, first let us goe to dinner?

Jessi. Nay, let me praise you while I have a stomack?

Loren. No pray thee, let it serve for table talke,
Then how so mere thou speakst mong other things,
I shall disgest it?

Jessi. Well, ile set you forth.   *Exit.*

Enter the Duke, the Magnificoes, Anthonio, Bassanio,
and Gratiano.

Duke. What, is *Anthonio* heere?

Antho. Ready, so please your grace?

Duke. I am sorry for thee, thou art come to aunswere
a stonie adversarie, an inhumaine wretch,
uncapable of pitty, voyd, and empty
from any dram of mercie.

Antho. I have heard
your grace hath tane great paines to quallifie
his rigorous course; but since he stands obdurate,
And that no lawfull meanes can carry me
out of his envies reach, I doe oppose
my patience to his furie, and am armd
to suffer with a quietnes of spirit,
the very tiranny and rage of his.

[88]

the Merchant of Venice

Duke. Goe one and call the Jew into the Court.
Salerio. He is ready at the dore, he comes my Lord.

Enter Shylocke.

Duke. Make roome, and let him stand before our face.
Shylocke the world thinks, and I thinke so to
that thou but leadest this fashion of thy mallice
to the last houre of act, and then tis thought
thowlt shew thy mercy and remorse more strange,
than is thy strange apparant cruelty;
and where thou now exacts the penalty,
which is a pound of this poore Merchants flesh,
thou wilt not onely loose the forfaiture,
but toucht with humaine gentlenes and love:
Forgive a moytie of the principall,
glauncing an eye of pitty on his losses
that have of late so hudled on his backe,
Enow to presse a royall Merchant downe;
And pluck comiseration of this states
from brassie bosomes and rough harts of flints,
from stubborne Turkes, and Tarters never traind
to offices of tender curtesie:
We all expect a gentle aunswere Jewe?
Jewe. I have possest your grace of what I purpose,
and by our holy Sabaoth have I sworne
to have the due and forfet of my bond,
if you deny it, let the danger light
upon your charter and your Citties freedome?
Youle aske me why I rather choose to have
a weight of carrion flesh, then to receave
three thousand ducats: Ile not aunswer that?
But say it is my humour, is it aunswerd?
What if my house be troubled with a Rat,
and I be pleasd to give ten thousand ducats
to have it baind? what, are you aunswerd yet?
Some men there are love not a gaping pigge?
Some that are mad if they behold a Cat?

[89]

And others when the bagpipe sings ith nose,
cannot containe their urine for affection.
Maisters of passion swayes it to the moode
of what it likes or loathes, now for your aunswer:
As there is no firme reason to be rendred
why he cannot abide a gaping pigge?
why he a harmelesse necessarie Cat?
why he a woollen bagpipe: but of force
must yeeld to such in evitable shame,
as to offend himselfe being offended:
So can I give no reason, nor I will not,
more then a lodgd hate, and a certaine loathing
I beare *Anthonio*, that *I* follow thus
a loosing sute against him? are you aunswered?

   Bass. This is no aunswer thou unfeeling man,
to excuse the currant of thy cruelty?

   Jewe. I am not bound to please thee with my answers?

   Bass. Doe all men kill the things they do not love?

   Jewe. Hates any man the thing he would not kill?

   Bass. Every offence is not a hate at first?

   Jewe. What wouldst thou have a serpent sting thee twice?

   Anth. I pray you think you question with the *Jewe*,
you may as well goe stand upon the Beach
and bid the maine flood bate his usuall height,
you may as well use question with the Woolfe,
why he hath made the Ewe bleake for the Lambe:
You may as well forbid the mountaine of Pines
to wag their high tops, and to make no noise
when they are fretten with the gusts of heaven:
You may as well doe any thing most hard
as seeke to soften that then which what's harder:
his Jewish hart? therefore I doe beseech you
make no moe offers, use no farther meanes,
but with all briefe and plaine conveniencie
let me have judgement, and the *Jewe* his will?

   Bass. For thy three thousand ducats heere is sixe?

   Jewe. If every ducat in sixe thousand ducats

were in sixe parts, and every part a ducat,
I would not draw them, *I* would have my bond?
   Duk. How shalt thou hope for mercy rendring none?
   Jewe. What judgment shall *I* dread doing no wrong?
you have among you many a purchast slave,
which like your Asses, and your Dogs and Mules
you use in abject and in slavish parts,
because you bought them, shall *I* say to you,
let them be free, marry them to your heires?
why sweat they under burthens, let their beds
be made as soft as yours, and let their pallats
be seasond with such viands, you will aunswer
the slaves are ours, so doe *I* aunswer you:
The pound of flesh which *I* demaund of him
is deerely bought, as mine and *I* will have it:
if you deny me, fie upon your Law,
there is no force in the decrees of Venice:
I stand for judgement, aunswer, shall I have it?
   Duke. Upon my power *I* may dismisse this Court,
unlesse *Bellario* a learned Doctor,
whome *I* have sent for to determine this
Come heere to day?
   Salerio. My Lord, heere stayes without
a messenger with letters from the Doctor,
new come from Padua?
   Duke. Bring us the letters? call the Messenger?
   Bass. Good cheere *Anthonio*? what man, courage yet:
The Jew shall have my flesh, blood, bones and all,
ere thou shalt loose for me one drop of blood?
   Antho. *I* am a tainted weather of the flocke,
meetest for death, the weakest kind of fruite
drops earliest to the ground, and so let me;
You cannot better be imployd *Bassanio*,
then to live still and write mine Epitaph?

Enter Nerrissa.

   Duke. Came you from Padua from *Bellario*?

[91]

Ner. From both? my L. *Bellario* greetes your grace?

Bass. Why doost thou whet thy knife so earnestly?

Jewe. To cut the forfaiture from that bankrout there?

Gratia. Not on thy soule: but on thy soule harsh Jew
thou makst thy knife keene: but no mettell can,
no, not the hangmans axe beare halfe the keenenesse
of thy sharpe envie; can no prayers pearce thee?

Jewe. No, none that thou hast wit enough to make.

Gratia. O be thou damnd, inexecrable dogge,
And for thy life let justice be accusd;
Thou almost mak'st me waver in my faith,
to hold opinion with *Pythagoras*,
that soules of Animalls infuse themselves
into the trunks of men: Thy currish spirit
governd a Woolfe, who hangd for humaine slaughter
even from the gallowes did his fell soule fleete,
and whilest thou layest in thy unhallowed dam;
infusd it selfe in thee: for thy desires
are wolvish, bloody, starv'd, and ravenous.

Jewe. Till thou canst raile the seale from off my bond,
Thou but offendst thy lungs to speake so loud:
Repaire thy wit good youth, or it will fall
to curelesse ruine. I stand heere for law.

Duke. This letter from *Bellario* doth commend
a young and learned Doctor to our Court:
Where is he?

Ner. He attendeth here hard by
to know your aunswer whether youle admit him.

Duke. With all my hart: some three or foure of you
goe give him curteous conduct to this place,
meane time the Court shall heare *Bellarios* letter.

Your Grace shall understand, that at the receit of your
letter I am very sicke, but in the instant that your messenger
came, in loving visitation was with me a young Doctor of
Rome, his name is *Balthazer*: *I* acquainted him with the cause
in controversie between the Jew and *Anthonio* the Merchant,

wee turnd ore many bookes together, hee is furnished with my opinion, which bettered with his owne learning, the greatnes whereof I cannot enough commend, comes with him at my importunitie, to fill up your graces request in my stead. *I* beseech you let his lacke of yeeres be no impediment to let him lacke a reverend estimation, for *I* never knew so young a body with so olde a head: I leave him to your gracious acceptance, whose tryall shal better publish his commendation.

Enter *Portia* for *Balthazer.*

Duke. You heare the learnd *Bellario* what he writes,
and heere I take it is the doctor come.
Give me your hand, come you from old *Bellario?*
    Portia. I did my Lord.
    Duke. You are welcome, take your place:
are you acquainted with the difference
that holds this present question in the Court.
    Portia. I am enformed throughly of the cause,
which is the Merchant here? and which the Jew?
    Duke. Anthonio and old *Shylocke,* both stand forth.
    Por. Is your name *Shylocke?*
    Jew. Shylocke is my name.
    Por. Of a strange nature is the sute you follow,
yet in such rule, that the Venetian law
cannot impugne you as you doe proceed.
You stand within his danger, doe you not.
    An. I, so he sayes.
    Por. Doe you confesse the bond?
    An. I doe.
    Por. Then must the Jew be mercifull.
    Shy. On what compulsion must I, tell me that.
    Por. The qualitie of mercie is not straind,
it droppeth as the gentle raine from heaven
upon the place beneath: it is twise blest,
it blesseth him that gives, and him that takes,
tis mightiest in the mightiest, it becomes

[93]

the throned Monarch better then his crowne.
His scepter showes the force of temporall power,
the attribut to awe and majestie,
wherein doth sit the dread and feare of Kings:
but mercie is above this sceptred sway,
it is enthroned in the harts of Kings,
it is an attribut to God himselfe;
and earthly power doth then show likest gods
when mercie seasons justice: therefore *Jew*,
though justice be thy plea, consider this,
that in the course of justice, none of us
should see salvation: we doe pray for mercy,
and that same prayer, doth teach us all to render
the deedes of mercie. I have spoke thus much
to mittigate the justice of thy plea,
which if thou follow, this strict Court of Venice
must needes give sentence gainst the Merchant there.

Shy. My deeds upon my head, I crave the law,
the penalty and forfaite of my bond.

Por. Is he not able to discharge the money?

Bass. Yes, heere I tender it for him in the Court,
yea twise the summe, if that will not suffise,
I will be bound to pay it ten times ore
on forfait of my hands, my head, my hart,
if this will not suffise, it must appeare
that malice beares downe truth. And *I* beseech you
wrest once the law to your authoritie,
to doe a great right, doe a little wrong,
and curbe this cruell devill of his will.

Por. It must not be, there is no power in Venice
can altar a decree established:
twill be recorded for a precedent,
and many an errour by the same example
will rush into the state, it cannot be.

Shy. A Daniell come to judgement: yea a Daniell.
O wise young Judge how *I* doe honour thee.

Por. I pray you let me looke upon the bond.

Shy. Heere tis most reverend doctor, here it is.

Por. Shylocke theres thrice thy money offred thee.

Shy. An oath, an oath, I have an oath in heaven,
shall I lay perjurie upon my soule?
Not not for Venice.

Por. Why this bond is forfait,
and lawfully by this the Jew may claime
a pound of flesh, to be by him cut off
neerest the Merchants hart: be mercifull,
take thrice thy money, bid me teare the bond.

Shy. When it is payd, according to the tenure.
It doth appeare you are a worthy judge,
you know the law, your exposition
hath beene most sound: *I* charge you by the law,
whereof you are a well deserving piller,
proceede to judgement: by my soule I sweare,
there is no power in the tongue of man
to alter me, *I* stay here on my Bond.

An. Most hartelie *I* doe beseech the Court
to give the judgement.

Por. Why than thus it is,
you must prepare your bosome for his knife.

Shy. O noble Judge, ô excellent young man.

Por. For the intent and purpose of the law
hath full relation to the penaltie,
which heere appeareth due upon the bond.

Jew. Tis very true: ô wise and upright Judge,
how much more elder art thou then thy lookes.

Por. Therefore lay bare your bosome.

Jew. I, his breast,
so sayes the bond, doth it not noble Judge?
Neerest his hart, those are the very words.

Por. It is so, are there ballance here to weigh the flesh?

Jew. I have them ready.

Por. Have by some Surgion *Shylocke* on your charge,
to stop his wounds, least he doe bleede to death.

Jew. Is it so nominated in the bond?

Por. It is not so exprest, but what of that?
Twere good you doe so much for charitie.

Jew. I cannot finde it, tis not in the bond.

Por. You Merchant, have you any thing to say?

Ant. But little; *I* am armd and well prepard,
give me your hand *Bassanio*, far you well,
greeve not that *I* am falne to this for you:
for heerein Fortune showes her selfe more kind
then is her custome: it is still her use
to let the wretched man out-live his wealth,
to view with hollow eye and wrinckled brow
an age of povertie: from which lingring pennance
of such misery doth she cut me of.
Commend me to your honourable wife,
tell her the processe of *Anthonios* end,
say how I lov'd you, speake me faire in death:
and when the tale is told, bid her be judge
whether *Bassanio* had not once a love:
Repent but you that you shall loose your friend
and he repents not that he payes your debt.
For if the *Jew* doe cut but deepe enough,
*I*le paye it instantly with all my hart.

Bass. Anthonio, I am married to a wife
which is as deere to me as life it selfe,
but life it selfe, my wife, and all the world,
are not with me esteemd above thy life.
I would loose all, I sacrifize them all
heere to this devill, to deliver you.

Por. Your wife would give you little thankes for that
if she were by to heare you make the offer.

Gra. I have a wife who *I* protest *I* love,
I would she were in heaven, so she could
intreate some power to change this currish Jew.

Ner. Tis well you offer it behind her back,
the wish would make else an unquiet house.

Jew. These be the christian husbands, *I* have a daughter
would any of the stocke of Barrabas

had beene her husband, rather then a Christian.
We trifle time, *I* pray thee pursue sentence.

   Por. A pound of that same Merchants flesh is thine,
the Court awards it, and the law doth give it.

   Jew. Most rightfull Judge.

   Por. And you must cut this flesh from off his breast,
the law alowes it, and the court awards it.

   Jew. Most learned Judge, a sentence, come prepare.

   Por. Tarry a little, there is some thing else,
this bond doth give thee heere no jote of blood,
the words expresly are a pound of flesh:
take then thy bond, take thou thy pound of flesh,
but in the cutting it, if thou doost shed
one drop of Christian blood, thy lands and goods
are by the lawes of Venice confiscate
unto the state of Venice.

   Gra. O upright Judge,
Marke Jew, ô learned *Judge.*

   Shy. Is that the law?

   Por. Thy selfe shall see the Act:
for as thou urgest justice, be assurd
thou shalt have justice more then thou desirst.

   Gra. O learned judge, mark *Jew,* a learned judge.

   Jew. I take this offer then, pay the bond thrice
and let the Christian goe.

   Bass. Heere is the money.

   Por. Soft, the Jew shal have all justice, soft no hast,
he shall have nothing but the penalty.

   Gra. O Jew, an upright Judge, a learned Judge.

   Por. Therefore prepare thee to cut of the flesh,
Shed thou no blood, nor cut thou lesse nor more
but just a pound of flesh: if thou tak'st more
or lesse then a just pound, be it but so much
as makes it light or heavy in the substance,
or the devision of the twentith part
of one poore scruple, nay if the scale doe turne
but in the estimation of a hayre,

thou dyest, and all thy goods are confiscate.

   Gra. A second Daniell, a Daniell Jew,
now infidell *I* have you on the hip.

   Por. Why doth the Jew pause, take thy forfaiture.

   Shy. Give me my principall, and let me goe.

   Bass. I have it ready for thee, here it is.

   Por. Hee hath refusd it in the open Court,
hee shall have meerely justice and his bond.

   Gra. A Daniell still say *I*, a second Daniell,
I thanke thee Jew for teaching me that word.

   Shy. Shall *I* not have barely my principall?

   Por. Thou shalt have nothing but the forfaiture
to be so taken at thy perrill Jew.

   Shy. Why then the devill give him good of it:
Ile stay no longer question.

   Por. Tarry Jew,
the law hath yet another hold on you.
It is enacted in the lawes of Venice,
if it be proved against an alien,
that by direct, or indirect attempts
he seeke the life of any Cittizen,
the party gainst the which he doth contrive,
shall seaze one halfe his goods, the other halfe
comes to the privie coffer of the State,
and the offenders life lies in the mercy
of the Duke onely, gainst all other voyce.
In which predicament I say thou standst:
for it appeares by manifest proceeding,
that indirectly, and directly to
thou hast contrived against the very life
of the defendant: and thou hast incurd
the danger formorly by me rehearst.
Downe therefore, and beg mercie of the Duke.

   Gra. Beg that thou maist have leave to hang thy selfe,
and yet thy wealth beeing forfait to the state,
thou hast not left the value of a cord,
therefore thou must be hangd at the states charge.

Duke. That thou shalt see the difference of our spirit
I pardon thee thy life before thou aske it:
for halfe thy wealth, it is *Anthonios,*
the other halfe comes to the generall state,
which humblenes may drive unto a fine.

Por. I for the state, not for *Anthonio.*

Shy. Nay, take my life and all, pardon not that,
you take my house, when you doe take the prop
that doth sustaine my house: you take my life
when you doe take the meanes whereby *I* live.

Por. What mercy can you render him *Anthonio?*

Gra. A halter gratis, nothing else for Godsake.

Anth. So please my Lord the Duke, & all the Court
to quit the fine for one halfe of his goods,
I am content: so he will let me have
the other halfe in use, to render it
upon his death unto the Gentleman
that lately stole his daughter.
Two things provided more, that for this favour
he presently become a Christian:
the other, that he doe record a gift
heere in the Court of all he dies possest
unto his sonne *Lorenzo* and his daughter.

Duke. He shall doe this, or else I doe recant
the pardon that I late pronounced heere.

Por. Art thou contented Jew? what dost thou say?

Shy. I am content.

Por. Clarke, draw a deede of gift.

Shy. I pray you give me leave to goe from hence,
I am not well, send the deede after me,
and I will signe it.

Duke. Get thee gone, but doe it.

Shy. In christning shalt thou have two Godfathers,
had I been judge, thou shouldst have had ten more,
to bring thee to the gallowes, not to the font.   *Exit.*

Duke. Sir I entreate you home with me to dinner.

Por. I humbly doe desire your Grace of pardon,

[99]

I must away this night toward Padua,
and it is meete I presently set forth.

   Duke. I am sorry that your leysure serves you not.
Anthonio, gratifie this gentleman,
for in my mind you are much bound to him.

Exit Duke and his traine.

   Bass. Most worthy gentleman, I and my friend
have by your wisedome been this day aquitted
of greevous penalties, in lewe whereof,
three thousand ducats due unto the *Jew*
wee freely cope your curtious paines withall.

   An. And stand indebted over and above
in love and service to you ever-more.

   Por. Hee is well payd that is well satisfied,
and I delivering you, am satisfied,
and therein doe account my selfe well payd,
my minde was never yet more mercinarie.
I pray you know me when we meete againe,
I wish you well, and so I take my leave.

   Bass. Deere sir, of force *I* must attempt you further,
take some remembrance of us as a tribute,
not as fee: graunt me two things I pray you,
not to deny me, and to pardon me.

   Por. You presse me farre, and therefore *I* wil yeeld,
give mee your gloves, Ile weare them for your sake,
and for your love ile take this ring from you,
doe not draw back your hand, ile take no more,
and you in love shall not denie me this?

   Bass. This ring good sir, alas it is a trifle,
I will not shame my selfe to give you this?

   Por. I will have nothing else but onely this,
and now me thinks I have a minde to it?

   Bass. There's more depends on this then on the valew,
the dearest ring in Venice will I give you,
and finde it out by proclamation,
onely for this I pray you pardon me?

[100]

Por. I see sir you are liberall in offers,
you taught me first to beg, and now me thinks
you teach me how a begger should be aunswerd.

Bass. Good sir, this ring was given me by my wife,
and when she put it on, she made me vowe
that I should neither sell, nor give, nor loose it.

Por. That scuse serves many men to save their gifts,
and if your wife be not a mad woman,
and know how well I have deserv'd this ring,
she would not hold out enemy for ever
for giving it to me: well, peace be with you.   *Exeunt.*

Anth. My L. *Bassanio*, let him have the ring,
let his deservings and my love withall
be valued gainst your wives commaundement.

Bass. Goe *Gratiano*, runne and over-take him,
give him the ring, and bring him if thou canst
unto *Anthonios* house, away, make hast.   *Exit Gratiano.*
Come, you and I will thither presently,
and in the morning early we will both
flie toward Belmont, come *Anthonio*.

                                        Exeunt.

Enter Nerrissa.

Por. Enquire the Jewes house out, give him this deed,
and let him signe it, weele away to night,
and be a day before our husbands home:
this deede will be well welcome to *Lorenzo*?

Enter Gratiano.

Grati. Faire sir, you are well ore-tane:
My L. *Bassanio* upon more advice,
hath sent you heere this ring, and doth intreate
your company at dinner.

Por. that cannot be;
his ring I doe accept most thankfully,
and so I pray you tell him: furthermore,
I pray you shew my youth old *Shylockes* house.

[101]

Gra. That will I doe.

Ner. Sir, *I* would speake with you:
Ile see if *I* can get my husbands ring
which I did make him sweare to keepe for ever.

Por. Thou maist I warrant, we shal have old swearing
that they did give the rings away to men;
but wele out-face them, and out-sweare them to:
away, make hast, thou knowst where I will tarry.

Ner. Come good sir, will you shew me to this house.

Enter Lorenzo and Jessica.

Lor. The moone shines bright. In such a night as this,
when the sweet winde did gently kisse the trees,
and they did make no noyse, in such a night
Troylus me thinks mounted the Trojan walls,
and sigh'd his soule toward the Grecian tents
where *Cressed* lay that night.

Jessi. In such a night
did *Thisbie* fearefully ore-trip the dewe,
and saw the Lyons shadow ere him selfe,
and ranne dismayed away.

Loren. In such a night
stoode *Dido* with a willow in her hand
upon the wilde sea banks, and waft her Love
to come againe to Carthage.

Jessi. In such a night
Medea gathered the inchanted hearbs
that did renew old *Eson.*

Loren. In such a night
did *Jessica* steale from the wealthy Jewe,
and with an unthrift love did runne from Venice,
as farre as Belmont.

Jessi. In such a night
did young *Lorenzo* sweare he loved her well,
stealing her soule with many vowes of faith,
and nere a true one.

Loren. In such a night

did pretty *Jessica* (like a little shrow)
slaunder her Love, and he forgave it her.
   Jessi. I would out-night you did no body come:
But harke, I heare the footing of a man.

Enter a Messenger.

   Loren. Who comes so fast in silence of the night?
   Messen. A friend?
   Loren. A friend, what friend, your name I pray you friend?
   Mess. Stephano is my name, and I bring word
my Mistres will before the breake of day
be heere at Belmont, she doth stray about
by holy crosses where she kneeles and prayes
for happy wedlock houres.
   Loren. Who comes with her?
   Mess. None but a holy Hermit and her mayd:
I pray you is my Maister yet returnd?
   Loren. He is not, nor we have not heard from him,
But goe we in I pray thee *Jessica*,
and ceremoniously let us prepare
some welcome for the Mistres of the house.   *Enter Clowne.*
   Clowne. Sola, sola: wo ha, ho sola, sola.
   Loren. Who calls?
   Clo. Sola, did you see M. *Lorenzo*, & Mr. *Lorenzo* sola, sola.
   Loren. Leave hollowing man, heere.
   Clowne. Sola, where, where?
   Loren. Heere?
   Clow. Tell him there's a Post come from my Maister, with
his horne full of good news, my Maister will be heere ere
morning sweete soule.
   Loren. Let's in, and there expect their comming.
And yet no matter: why should we goe in.
My friend *Stephen*, signifie I pray you
within the house, your mistres is at hand,
and bring your musique foorth into the ayre.
How sweet the moone-light sleepes upon this banke,
heere will we sit, and let the sounds of musique

[103]

creepe in our eares soft stilnes, and the night
become the tutches of sweet harmonie:
sit *Jessica*, looke how the floore of heaven
is thick inlayed with pattens of bright gold,
there's not the smallest orbe which thou beholdst
but in his motion like an Angell sings,
still quiring to the young eyde Cherubins;
such harmonie is in immortall soules,
but whilst this muddy vesture of decay
dooth grosly close it in, we cannot heare it:
Come hoe, and wake *Diana* with a himne,
with sweetest tutches pearce your mistres eare,
and draw her home with musique.   *play Musique.*
  Jessi. I am never merry when I heare sweet musique.
  Loren. The reason is your spirits are attentive:
for doe but note a wild and wanton heard
or race of youthfull and unhandled colts
fetching mad bounds, bellowing and neghing loude,
which is the hote condition of their blood,
if they but heare perchance a trumpet sound,
or any ayre of musique touch their eares,
you shall perceave them make a mutuall stand,
their savage eyes turn'd to a modest gaze,
by the sweet power of musique: therefore the Poet
did faine that Orpheus drew trees, stones, and floods.
Since naught so stockish hard and full of rage,
but musique for the time doth change his nature,
the man that hath no musique in himselfe,
nor is not moved with concord of sweet sounds,
is fit for treasons, stratagems, and spoiles,
the motions of his spirit are dull as night,
and his affections darke as *Terebus*:
let no such man be trusted: marke the musique.

Enter Portia and Nerrissa.

  Por. That light we see is burning in my hall:
how farre that little candell throwes his beames,

[104]

so shines a good deede in a naughty world.

   Ner. When the moone shone we did not see the candle?

   Por. So dooth the greater glory dim the lesse,
a substitute shines brightly as a King
untill a King be by, and then his state
empties it selfe, as doth an inland brooke
into the maine of waters: musique harke.

   Ner. It is your musique Madame of the house?

   Por. Nothing is good I see without respect,
me thinks it sounds much sweeter then by day?

   Ner. Silence bestowes that vertue on it Madam?

   Por. The Crow doth sing as sweetly as the Larke
when neither is attended: and I thinke
the Nightingale if she should sing by day
when every Goose is cackling, would be thought
no better a Musition then the Renne?
How many things by season, seasond are
to their right prayse, and true perfection:
Peace, how the moone sleepes with Endimion,
and would not be awak'd.

   Loren. That is the voyce,
or I am much deceav'd of *Portia*.

   Por. He knowes me as the blind man knowes the Cuckoe
by the bad voyce?

   Loren. Deere Lady welcome home?

   Por. We have bin praying for our husbands welfare,
which speed we hope the better for our words:
are they return'd?

   Loren. Madam, they are not yet:
but there is come a Messenger before
to signifie their comming?

   Por. Goe in *Nerrissa*.
Give order to my servants, that they take
no note at all of our being absent hence,
nor you *Lorenzo*, *Jessica* nor you.

   Loren. Your husband is at hand, I heare his trumpet,
we are no tell-tales Madame, feare you not.

[105]

Por. This night me thinks is but the day light sicke,
it lookes a little paler, tis a day,
such as the day is when the sunne is hid.

Enter Bassanio, Anthonio, Gratiano, and their
followers.

Bass. We should hold day with the Antipodes,
if you would walke in absence of the sunne.
Por. Let me give light, but let me not be light,
for a light wife doth make a heavie husband,
and never be *Bassanio* so for me,
But God sort all: you are welcome home my Lord.
Bass. I thank you Madam, give welcome to my friend,
this is the man, this is *Anthonio*,
to whom I am so infinitely bound.
Por. You should in all sence be much bound to him,
for as I heare he was much bound for you.
Anth. No more then I am well acquitted of.
Por. Sir, you are very welcome to our house:
it must appeare in other wayes then words,
therefore I scant this breathing curtesie.
Gra. By yonder moone I sweare you doe me wrong,
infaith I gave it to the *Judges Clarke,*
would he were gelt that had it for my part,
since you doe take it Love so much at hart.
Por. A quarrell hoe already, what's the matter?
Grati. About a hoope of gold, a paltry ring
that she did give me, whose posie was
for all the world like Cutlers poetry
upon a knife, *Love me, and leave me not.*
Ner. What talke you of the posie or the valew:
You swore to me when I did give you,
that you would weare it till your houre of death,
and that it should lie with you in your grave,
though not for me, yet for your vehement oathes,
you should have beene respective and have kept it.
Gave it a Judges Clarke: no Gods my Judge

the Clarke will nere weare haire ons face that had it.

Gra. He will, and if he live to be a man.

Nerrissa. I, if a woman live to be a man.

Gra. Now by this hand I gave it to a youth,
a kind of boy, a little scrubbed boy,
no higher then thy selfe, the Judges Clarke,
a prating boy that begd it as a fee,
I could not for my hart deny it him.

Por. You were to blame, I must be plaine with you,
to part so slightly with your wives first gift,
a thing stuck on with oaths upon your finger,
and so riveted with faith unto your flesh.
I gave my Love a ring, and made him sweare
never to part with it, and heere he stands:
I dare be sworne for him he would not leave it,
nor pluck it from his finger, for the wealth
that the world maisters. Now in faith *Gratiano*
you give your wife too unkind a cause of griefe,
and twere to me I should be mad at it.

Bass. Why I were best to cut my left hand off,
and sweare I lost the ring defending it.

Gra. My Lord *Bassanio* gave his ring away
unto the Judge that begd it, and indeede
deserv'd it to: and then the boy his Clarke
that tooke some paines in writing, he begd mine,
and neither man nor maister would take ought
but the two rings.

Por What ring gave you my Lord?
Not that I hope which you receav'd of me.

Bass. If I could add a lie unto a fault,
I would deny it: but you see my finger
hath not the ring upon it, it is gone.

Por. Even so voyd is your false hart of truth.
By heaven I will nere come in your bed
untill I see the ring?

Ner. Nor I in yours
till I againe see mine?

Bass. Sweet *Portia*,
if you did know to whom I gave the ring,
if you did know for whom *I* gave the ring,
and would conceave for what *I* gave the ring,
and how unwillingly I left the ring,
when naught would be accepted but the ring,
you would abate the strength of your displeasure?

Por. If you had knowne the vertue of the ring,
or halfe her worthines that gave the ring,
or your owne honour to containe the ring,
you would not then have parted with the ring:
what man is there so much unreasonable
if you had pleasd to have defended it
with any termes of zeale: wanted the modesty
to urge the thing held as a ceremonie:
Nerrissa teaches me what to beleeve,
ile die for't, but some woman had the ring?

Bass. No by my honour Madam, by my soule
no woman had it, but a civill Doctor,
which did refuse three thousand ducats of me,
and begd the ring, the which I did denie him,
and sufferd him to goe displeasd away,
even he that had held up the very life
of my deere friend. What should *I* say sweet Lady,
I was inforc'd to send it after him,
I was beset with shame and curtesie,
my honour would not let ingratitude
so much besmere it: pardon me good Lady,
for by these blessed candels of the night,
had you been there, I think you would have begd
the ring of me to give the worthy Doctor?

Por. Let not that Doctor ere come neere my house
since he hath got the jewell that I loved,
and that which you did sweare to keepe for me,
I will become as liberall as you,
Ile not deny him any thing I have,
no, not my body, nor my husbands bed:

[108]

Know him I shall, I am well sure of it.
Lie not a night from home. Watch me like Argos,
if you doe not, if I be left alone,
now by mine honour which is yet mine owne,
ile have that Doctor for mine bedfellow.

Nerrissa. And I his Clark: therefore be well advisd
how you doe leave me to mine owne protection.

Gra. Well doe you so: let not me take him then,
for if I doe, ile mar the young Clarks pen.

Anth. I am th'unhappy subject of these quarrells.

Por. Sir, greeve not you, you are welcome notwithstanding.

Bass. Portia, forgive me this enforced wrong,
and in the hearing of these many friends
I sweare to thee, even by thine owne faire eyes
wherein I see my selfe.

Por. Marke you but that?
*I*n both my eyes he doubly sees himselfe:
In each eye one, sweare by your double selfe,
and there's an oath of credite.

Bass. Nay, but heare me.
Pardon this fault, and by my soule I sweare
I never more will breake an oath with thee.

Anth. I once did lend my body for his wealth,
which but for him that had your husbands ring
had quite miscaried. *I* dare be bound againe,
my soule upon the forfet, that your Lord
will never more breake faith advisedly.

Por. Then you shall be his surety: give him this,
and bid him keepe it better then the other.

Antho. Here Lord *Bassanio*, sweare to keepe this ring.

Bass. By heaven it is the same I gave the Doctor.

Por. I had it of him: pardon me *Bassanio*,
for by this ring the Doctor lay with me.

Nerrissa. And pardon me my gentle *Gratiano*,
for that same scrubbed boy the Doctors Clarke
in liew of this, last night did lie with me.

Grati. Why this is like the mending of high wayes

in Sommer where the wayes are faire enough?
What, are we cuckolds ere we have deserv'd it.

Por. Speake not so grosly, you are all amaz'd;
Heere is a letter, reade it at your leasure,
It comes from Padua from *Bellario*,
there you shall finde that *Portia* was the Doctor,
Nerrissa there her Clarke. *Lorenzo* heere
shall witnes I set foorth as soone as you,
and even but now returnd: *I* have not yet
enterd my house. *Anthonio* you are welcome,
and I have better newes in store for you
than you expect: unseale this letter soone,
there you shall finde three of your Argosies
are richly come to harbour sodainly.
You shall not know by what strange accident
I chaunced on this letter.

Antho. *I* am dumb?

Bass. Were you the Doctor, and *I* knew you not?

Gra. Were you the Clark that is to make me cuckold.

Ner. *I* but the Clarke that never meanes to doe it,
unlesse he live untill he be a man.

Bass. (Sweet Doctor) you shall be my bedfellow,
when *I* am absent then lie with my wife.

An. (Sweet Lady) you have given me life and lyving,
for heere *I* reade for certaine that my ships
are safely come to Rode.

Por. How now *Lorenzo*?
my Clarke hath some good comforts to for you.

Ner. *I*, and ile give them him without a fee.
There doe *I* give to you and *Jessica*
from the rich *Jewe*, a speciall deede of gift
after his death, of all he dies possest of.

Loren. Faire Ladies, you drop Manna in the way
of starved people.

Por. It is almost morning,
and yet *I* am sure you are not satisfied
of these events at full. Let us goe in,

and charge us there upon intergotories,
and we will aunswer all things faithfully.

    Gra. Let it be so, the first intergotory
that my *Nerrissa* shall be sworne on, is,
whether till the next night she had rather stay,
or goe to bed now being two houres to day:
But were the day come, *I* should wish it darke
till *I* were couching with the Doctors Clarke.
Well, while *I* live, ile feare no other thing
so sore, as keeping safe *Nerrissas* ring.

                                    Exeunt.

FINIS.

Endnotes

These notes are not intended to supply readers with every possible aid to understanding *The most excellent Historie of the Merchant of Venice*. They focus on special features of the play as a play, on obscurities caused by old spelling and archaisms, and on textual problems unique to the 1600 Quarto. It is assumed that the advanced readers and students who will use the *Shakespearean Originals* series will be largely familiar with common Elizabethan usages, contractions or commonplaces.

Page 32
The most excellent Historie: the play is a close adaptation of a medieval Italian *novella* by Ser Giovanni. The term *history* is, in Elizabethan culture, still loosely employed to denote a story of any kind. By 1623 the Folio editors felt it necessary to qualify this title as potentially misleading, replacing it with the running title of the 1600 Quarto, *The comicall History*. But see the Introduction (pp. 14–15) for the deliberately misleading nature of the Quarto's subtitle.

Page 37
I am to learne: and such a want-wit sadnes
*   makes of mee,*
That I have much adoe to know my selfe: repeated in Q2 (1619), and Folio (1623); Q3 (1637) alters to now accepted lineation, in which 'I am to learne' stands alone as a half-line. Q1's arrangement, however, is visually poignant, since it isolates *sadnes* as Anthonio's mysterious essence.

Argosies: merchant ships.

Signiors: noblemen (the *signoria* of Venice), in contrast to *Burgars*, wealthy citizens, and in greater contrast to *petty traffiquers*, common traders.

Pageants: ornate floats in street processions.

over-peere: look down on; there is a metaphor of class hierarchy here.

cursie: curtsey, a gesture of social submission, the female equivalent of a bow.

had I such venture forth: if I had such a risky capital venture afloat. *Venture* is one of the terms that link the Belmont and Venice (or love and money) plots as analogous rather than contrasting.

Piring: looking closely; a different word from *peer*, with the preceding *over-peere* and the following *peers* (piers) Q1 thus offers a three-way word-play.

rodes: anchorages.

Page 38

ague: fever.

Andrew: an allusion to a famous Spanish galleon (the *San Andres*) captured in Essex's Cadiz expedition in June 1596; a *terminus a quo* for dating the play.

docks: Q1 in probable error for *dockt* (Rowe's emendation).

Vayling: lowering sail.

bottome: ship's hull; the phrase had proverbial status; cf. 'Don't put all your eggs in one basket'.

Janus: the Roman god of doorways, one of his heads looking to the past and one to the future.

Page 39

Nestor: the aged counsellor to the Greeks in the *Iliad*; hence a figure for gravity.

occasion: opportunity; Anthonio suggests Salarino has given an insincere excuse for departure.

strange: cool, unfriendly; this whole exchange is strange in the other sense, suggesting social friction. Anthonio and Bassanio belong to the *signoria*, the others do not.

You have too much . . . much care: you take the world too seriously; those who do so lose touch with it.

Alablaster: alabaster, a white stone used for funeral effigies.

Jaundies: jaundice, thought to be caused by depression.

Page 40

creame and mantle: thicken into impassivity; the figure combines sitting milk and stagnant water.

Endnotes

If they should speake . . . brothers fooles: an allusion to Matthew 5:22: 'whosoever shall say unto his brother . . . thou fool shall be in danger of hell fire'. Those who acquire a reputation for wisdom by maintaining silence would be recognised as fools as soon as they spoke, hence putting a strain on the generosity of their audience.

gudgin: gudgeon, an easily caught fish, hence a figure for gullibility.

moe: more in number, as distinct from 'more' in other senses.

Far you well: farewell; cf. Gratiano's previous *faryewell*.

for this geare: either 'in response to your arguments' or, turning to Bassanio, 'for the matter I know you wish to raise'.

togue: Q1 in error for *tongue*; Q2 corrects. Gratiano crudely asserts that reticence is only acceptable in a dried calf's tongue (i.e. withered penis, old man) or an unmarketable woman (old maid).

It is that any thing now: a somewhat ambiguous response to Gratiano's departure, tempting editors to emend.

How much . . . continuance: how much I have reduced my net worth by living rather ostentatiously beyond my means.

Page 41

make mone to be abridg'd From such a noble rate: complain of having to cut back on my high lifestyle.

come fairely of from . . . gagd: honourably to discharge the great debts I have incurred in my rather too prodigal past.

prodigall: spendthrift; another theme word of this play here makes its first significant appearance.

And from your love . . . debts I owe: and your love guarantees that I may freely unburden myself to you of all my plans as to how to clear my debts. The need for extensive glossing in this speech, untypical of this play, suggests that Bassanio is too embarrassed to be straightforward.

My purse, my person: those who suspect Anthonio of homosexual love for Bassanio would recognise in this jingle a *double-entendre* on *purse* (testicles).

occasions: needs.

To wind about my love with circumstance: to approach me so deviously.

In making question of my uttermost: in doubting how far my generosity extends.

[114]

Endnotes

richly left: has inherited a great fortune.

Catos daughter, Brutus Portia: daughter of the tribune Cato and wife to Brutus, hero of republicanism, Portia was famous for intelligence and integrity in her own right.

golden fleece . . . many Jasons: an allusion to the *Argonautica*, Jason's quest in the ship named the Argo to steal the legendary Golden Fleece from Colchis on the Black Sea. The similarity between *Jason* and *Jacob* as entrepreneurs from different cultures should not be overlooked.

thrift: profit, success; the third of the theme words connecting the romantic and financial plots, and a favourite term with Shylock.

commoditie: goods, property.

rackt: stretched.

of my trust . . . sake: on the strength of my financial credit or my personal character.

it is no meane . . . in the meane: it is no small happiness to achieve the golden mean between having too much and too little.

competencie: just enough.

Good sentences: wise sayings.

divine: clergyman.

will . . . will: the desires of a living daughter are restrained by her dead father's dying wish, as laid down in his will. Portia here introduces, by punning, the philosophical problem of the limits on personal choice and freedom that both plots exemplify.

levell at: take aim at, guess.

Neopolitane: of Naples; Q2 corrects to *Neapolitane*.

Countie: Count.

Palentine: Q2 corrects to Palatine. The Palatine was an area of the old German empire under the control of the Palsgrave, Count (or Elector) Palatine. The Palsgrave Ludovic, a Lutheran, had visited England in the 1580s.

& you will not have me, choose: if you will not have me, that's up to you.

weeping Phylosopher: Heraclitus of Ephesus, who was notoriously melancholy, in contrast to the laughing philosopher Democritus.

Endnotes

Trassell: throstle, thrush.

have a poore pennieworth in the English: speak very little English.

round hose: padded breeches.

his suretie: his guarantor. In this mock-anticipation of the money plot, the French, traditionally supporters of the Scots in their struggles against the English, stand in the same relation to the Scots as will Anthonio to Bassanio, 'seald' under a bond to deliver (or perhaps to receive) a second box on the ear when the debt comes due.

beast . . . beast: a joke that depends on the homonymic quality of 'best' and 'beast', working against the antithetical quality of 'best' and 'worst', 'man' and 'beast'.

the worst fall that ever fell: even if the worst happens.

Reynishe: Rhine wine, i.e. hock.

You neede not feare . . . the having: there is no danger of your having to marry any of these; Nerrissa now reveals that she has been merely teasing Portia, since she has known all along that the objects of their scorn are no longer suitors.

then: printed as *the* in Q1.

Sibilla: The Sibyl of Cumae, a prophetess condemned by Appollo's ambiguous gift to an unbearably long life.

Diana: goddess of chastity.

foure strangers: See Introduction, p. 17.

sirra goe before: whiles we shut the gate upon one wooer, another knocks at the doore: this absorption of the doggerel verse by the prose that precedes it is repeated in all Qs and F.

ducates: originally 'coins of the duke', this Venetian gold currency dated from the thirteenth century. By Shakespeare's time, a ducat would have been worth about 4s 8d.

I: aye.

a good man: his credit is good. The ambiguity allows Bassanio to misunderstand Shylock.

Endnotes

in supposition: speculative.

Ryalta: in error for *Rialto*, as later in Q1. The Rialto was the Venetian Exchange.

rats . . . Pyrats: the original spelling and pronunciation permits Shylock to make a joke.

to smell porke: in Judaism, eating pork is forbidden.

the Nazarit: Jesus of Nazareth. The reference is to Matthew 8:28.

Page 47

publican: tax-collector.

usance: another euphemism for usury.

catch . . . upon the hip: catch him at a disadvantage; the figure is from wrestling.

thrift: here used both for *profit*, and as a euphemism for *interrest*, a term which Shylock prefers not to use.

debating . . . present store: reckoning how much cash I have on hand.

months: months' credit.

excesse: interest.

ripe: urgent.

is hee . . . ye would: Anthonio turns to Bassanio and asks: 'Does he already know how much you want?'

I, I: aye, aye.

Upon advantage: upon interest.

When Jacob . . . and those were Jacobs: Genesis 30 is the source for this story, whereby Shylock justifies simultaneously making money 'breed' by taking interest and a certain amount of cunning therein. The figure of money breeding originated with Aristotle, whose condemnation of it as unnatural (*De Republica*, Book 1) was the origin of Christian anti-usury thought and legislation.

Abram: Abraham.

his wise mother . . . in his behalf: an allusion to Genesis 27, where Rebecca, Jacob's mother, deceives her blind husband Isaac into giving his blessing, the 'birthright' due to the elder son, Esau, to the younger one she loves better. By covering Jacob's hands with the skins of kids, and thereby

Endnotes

making 'smooth' Jacob feel like 'hairy' Esau, Rebecca started Jacob on his career as the Old Testament's most cunning hero.

Page 48

    compremyzd: agreed (literally, had promised together).

    eanelings: newborn lambs.

    streakt and pied: striped and spotted.

    hier: wages.

    ranck: in heat.

    work of generation: mating.

    pyld: pilled, an old form of peeled.

    deede of kind: mating.

    fulsome: full (of sex).

    Fall: drop, give birth to.

    rated: berated.

Page 49

    badge: metaphorical and literal, since Venetian Jews were required to wear a yellow badge.

    spet: spit.

    gaberdine: long cloak, associated with Jews in stage tradition.

    voyde your rume: spit.

    foote . . . curre: kick me as you would shove a strange dog.

    sute: request.

    for when did your friendship take A breede for barraine mettaile of his friend: since when did friendship insist that his friend make his barren metal breed for him?

    doyte: a trivial sum.

    single: bearing only your single signature.

Page 50

    left . . . unthriftie knave: which I have left in the unreliable care of a careless servant.

    gentle: the first of several puns on *gentle/Gentile*.

Endnotes

Page 51

tawnie: brown-skinned (as opposed to black).

complexion: colour of my skin.

liverie: the uniform worn by a nobleman's retinue.

Phoebus: the sun (Apollo).

make incyzion for your love: compete for your love by cutting ourselves.

this aspect . . . the valiant: this my appearance has made bold men afraid.

nice direction: discrimination. Portia claims she is not, like most young women, influenced by looks alone. But compare her contemptuous farewell to Morocco later.

scanted: restricted.

As any commer I have look'd on yet: but we have just heard what she thinks of those who have preceded him.

the Sophy: the Shah of Persia.

the Sultan Solyman: Soliman the Magnificent of Turkey. These persons were real, but the events alluded to are unhistorical.

Page 52

If Hercules . . . the weaker hand: if Hercules (the strongest hero in the ancient world) throws the dice with his servant Lychas to see which is the better man, luck may make the weaker man throw the higher number.

Alcides: the Greek name for Hercules. Here Morocco refers to a later phase in the legend, where Lychas brings his master the poisoned shirt that makes him mad with pain.

Nor will not: Morocco elliptically agrees to abide by the conditions.

serve me: permit me; in what follows, however, where Launcelet 'imagines himself the central character of a morality play' (Brown), his conscience argues *against* leaving.

coragious: encouraging.

fia: Off you go!

something smack . . . kinde of tast: three variants on the idea that old Gobbo had disreputable inclinations.

bouge: budge.

[119]

Endnotes

incarnation: incarnate, made flesh. The word is both the first of Launcelet's many malapropisms, and, since the Incarnation refers primarily to Christ, blasphemous.

Gobbo: for the difference between Jobbe and Gobbo, see Introduction, p. 18.

sand-blinde . . . gravell blinde: half-blind, much more than half-blind; 'sand' is from Old English 'sam-', half; but Launcelet takes it literally, and, knowing that 'stone-blind' means fully blind, invents 'gravel-blind' as somewhere between the two.

try confusions: Shakespeare's joke, not Launcelet's; to try conclusions means to experiment; Launcelet has the wrong word; and yet it is also clearly the right word for what follows. Q2 misses the point and emends to 'conclusions'.

Be Gods sonties: by God's saints.

raise the waters: bring tears to his eyes.

ergo: therefore (Latin); an academic term inappropriate in this conversation.

ant: and it.

sisters three: the Fates.

hovell post: the central post supporting a hut.

muder: in error for *murder*; emended to 'Murther' in Q2.

philhorse: carthorse, from the 'fills' or shafts of the cart.

lost: in error for 'last'; emended in Q2.

you may tell . . . with my ribs: back to front: properly, you can count every rib I have with your fingers; yet traditional stage business has Launcelet spread out his fingers to represent his ribs.

infection: Old Gobbo's mistake for 'affection', 'desire'.

catercosins: mealtime companions, close friends.

frutifie: Launcelet's mistake for 'certify'.

impertinent: Launcelet's mistake for 'pertinent', relating to.

Endnotes

Page 56

defect: Old Gobbo's mistake for 'effect'.

preferd . . . preferment: recommended you for promotion, if it is a promotion.

The old proverb: 'The grace of God is gear enough.' Launcelet 'parts' it between Shylock and Bassanio.

garded: braided; fools' costumes were especially heavily braided.

table: part of the palm of the hand.

a leven: eleven.

comming in: only a beginning.

scapes: escapes, adventures.

for this gere: for this business.

in the twinkling: in a moment; usually with 'of an eye'.

Page 57

to rude: too uncivilised.

Parts: characteristics.

liberall: free, undisciplined.

misconstred: misconstrued, misunderstood.

sad ostent: display of gravity.

Page 58

exhibit: Launcelet's mistake for 'inhibit'.

heynous: serious.

quaintly ordered: elegantly designed.

break up: break open.

it shal seeme to signifie: it will tell you something; an absurdly pompous way of putting it.

faire hand . . . faire hand: Lorenzo plays on the identity between Jessica's 'fine handwriting' and her 'beautiful hand'.

Page 59

maske: a formal entertainment featuring dancers; often the participants wore actual masks.

crosse her foote: trip her up.

Endnotes

faithlesse: outside the Christian faith.

gurmandize: eat like a glutton.

rend apparraile out: wear out clothes.

Page 60

a bruing towards: threatening.

reproch: Launcelet's mistake for 'approach'; but the error makes psychological sense, as Shylock's answer reveals.

black monday: Easter Monday.

wry-neckt Fiffe: the fife (a high-pitched wind instrument) is played with the head turned sideways.

varnisht: painted.

casements: windows.

fopprie: foppery, foolishness.

no minde of: no desire for.

    there will come a Christian by
will be worth a Jewes eye.
So Q1; Q2 aligns the couplet in left margin. 'Jewes' was probably pronounced 'Jewess'.

Hagar's offspring: Hagar was a bondwoman, servant to Sarah, Abraham's wife. Her son by Abraham was Ishmael, who became a figure (and justification) for all subsequent slaves and servants.

Page 61

patch: fool.

do as I bid you, shut dores after you, fast bind, fast find.
a proverbe never stale in thriftie minde: So in Q1, F.
Q2 relines:
Do as I bid you, shut doores after you,
Fast binde, fast finde,
A Proverbe never stale in thrifty minde.

penthouse: projecting upper storey.

younger: younger son, as in the parable of the Prodigal Son.

skarfed: wearing sails, like scarves.

strumpet: prostitute.

[122]

Endnotes

Page 62

garnish: adornment.

guild: literally, provide; metaphorically, gild, cover with gold.

Page 64

Hircanion: a famous wilderness south of the Caspian Sea.

ribb: encase.

serecloth: a shroud (made of waxed cloth).

tride: guaranteed pure.

Page 65

insculpt: engraved.

death: a skull.

complexion: an ironic echo of Morocco's opening appeal.

Gondylo: gondola, the distinctive Venetian canal boat.

Page 66

stones: a sexual *double-entendre*; *stones* can mean testicles. So also can *jewels*, as in 'the family jewels'.

fraught: loaded.

slumber: editors usually accept Q2's substitution of 'slubber', make a mess of; but the word sounds too gross for Anthonio's sensibility.

riping: ripening.

faire ostents . . . become you there: such displays of love as will be necessary or appropriate at the time.

Page 67

affection wondrous sencible: remarkably visible emotion.

quicken . . . heavines: alleviate this gloom he seems so committed to.

election: choice.

nuptiall rights . . . solemniz'd: marriage rites be performed.

addrest: prepared.

Page 68

Marlet: swift or house-martin.

Endnotes

force and rode of casualty: within the power and the reach of disaster.

jumpe with: go along with.

cosen: cheat.

cover . . . stand bare: keep their hats on that now doff them (in deference to others).

gleaned: sorted out.

chaft: chaff.

Page 69

judement: in error for 'judgement'; Q2 emends.

Iwis: certainly.

you are sped: you are done for.

wroath: ruth, misfortune.

moath: moth.

deliberate: reasoning elaborately.

sensible regreets: material greetings.

commends . . . breath: commendations and courteous speech.

Page 70

Post: messenger.

it lives there uncheckt: there is a persistent and uncontradicted rumour.

the Goodwins: notorious sandbanks off the coast of Kent.

gossip: old friend.

knapt Ginger: chewed ginger root.

slips of prolixity: lapses into talk for its own sake.

wings: Jessica's boy's costume.

flidge: old form of *fledged*, mature enough to fly. Q2 has *fledged*.

complexion: nature.

dam: mother (with a pun on the *damnd* that follows).

carrion: corpse.

rebels it at these yeeres: Solanio pretends that Shylock's reference to his rebellious flesh acknowledged an erection.

[124]

Endnotes

rennish: Rhine wine (hock), hence white.

dementions: dimensions.

Enter *Tuball*: repeated in error; corrected in Q2.

Franckford: Frankfurt in Germany; the site of a famous annual jewellery market.

hearsed: in her coffin.

breake: go bankrupt.

Turkies: turquoise.

fee me . . . before: hire me a sheriff's officer, engage him a fortnight before (the due date).

quallity: manner.

naughty: worthless.

and so . . . not I: and so if it should turn out that I, although yours in feeling, cannot be yours in fact, let Fortune be damned for it, not I.

peize: weigh down, slow down.

ech: eke out.

I but: Aye but.

Alcides . . . Sea-monster: this, the third allusion to Hercules, alludes to his rescue of Hesione, daughter of the king of Troy, from the sea-monster to which, one after another, the Trojan maidens were sacrificed.

I stand for sacrifice: literally, I represent the sacrificial victim; but in another sense Portia is both giving Bassanio a hint about which casket to choose and speaking to the larger moral themes of the play.

Dardanian: Trojan.

bleared visages: tear-stained faces.

Song: It has been argued that the text of the song (by subliminally suggesting, through its rhymes, the lead casket) also constitutes a hint to Bassanio.

Endnotes

fancie: attraction (as in the contemporary 'I fancy you').

stayers of sand: either *stairs*, or *stays*, ropes.

lyvers: the liver was supposed to be the organ of courage.

excrement: exterior growth.

redoubted: having a reputation for heroism.

purchast by the weight: bought by the pound.

Page 76

guiled: dangerous.

Indian: dark-skinned (cf. Morocco's *complexion*, above p. 51).

Hard food for Midas: Apollo granted King Midas his wish that everything he touched be turned to gold. Unfortunately, this applied equally to his food (and his daughter).

common drudge: general servant; a reference to silver's mundane role as the common coinage.

shyddring: shuddering.

tyntrap: to entrap.

Page 77

unfurnisht: unmatched; or, perhaps, unfinished.

continent: container.

by note: with a legal note of what is owed.

confirmd, signd, ratified: more legal language.

livings: possessions.

Page 78

vantage: opportunity, occasion.

blent: blended.

wild of nothing: a meaningless babble.

You lov'd . . . for intermission: the original punctuation here is misleading. Gratiano means that he has been just as businesslike in his courtship as has his master.

[126]

Endnotes

Page 75

rough: roof (of the mouth); Q2 supplies *roof*.

play . . . first boy: make a wager with them we will be the first to produce a son.

stake down . . . stake downe: Nerrissa asks if they will place their money on the table; Gratiano chooses to answer by a sexual *double-entrendre* – the 'stake' will need to be erect for them to win.

Page 80

royall Merchant: an allusion to the golden days of Venetian trade, when the *signoria* were proud to be merchants.

shrowd: shrewd, painful.

meere enemie: mortal enemy.

Page 81

impeach: casts slurs upon.

Magnificoes of greatest port: the Venetians of highest rank and authority.

best conditiond: most good-natured.

the auncient Romaine honour: a reference to the integrity on which the great Roman citizens of antiquity prided themselves.

Por. What . . . bond. One line in all Quartos. F corrects.

deface: cancel.

through: perhaps intended to be pronounced *throrough*.

Page 82

no bed . . . us twain: another promise that Bassanio will not keep.

phanges: fangs.

naughtie: useless.

Page 83

bootlesse: of no help.

commoditie: convenience, rights.

impeach: discredit.

bated: abated, reduced (in weight).

true conceite . . . amitie: an accurate concept of divine friendship.

Endnotes

Page 84

then customarie bountie can enforce you: than your usual generosity can make you.

egall: equal. Behind this speech lies the Renaissance theory of friendship derived from Aristotle's *Ethics*.

lyniaments: limbs, features.

husbandry and mannage: housekeeping and management.

Page 85

Mantua: in error for Padua.

imagin'd speede: with all speed imaginable.

Tranect: perhaps a misreading of *traject*, from *traghetto*, ferry.

accomplished . . . lacke: equipped with penises; a Freudian joke *avant la lettre*.

accoutered: dressed.

betweene . . . boy: as if my voice were in process of breaking.

quaint: cunning; but also, perhaps, with the older sexual meaning.

doe withall: avoid it.

Page 86

lewd interpreter: foolish (or lascivious) interpreter; Portia's comment applies better to her previous speech than to Nerrissa's innocent question.

feare you: fear for you.

a good chere: be cheerful.

bastard: conceived out of wedlock.

neither: too.

Scilla . . . Caribdis: Scylla and Charybdis, the legendary perils on each side of the straits of Messina (as in *Odyssey* 12).

enow: enough.

we shall . . . for mony: soon money won't buy a rasher (of bacon) to put on the fire.

Page 87

out: friends no longer.

Moore . . . more: a conventional pun, here playing on the enlargements of pregnancy.

[128]

Endnotes

stomacks: appetites.

cover . . . cover: Launcelet plays on the two meanings of the word, to set the table and to put one's hat on (instead of doffing it in deference to one's master).

quarrelling with occasion: taking every opportunity to be contrary.

humors and conceites: whims and fancies.

O deare discretion: Oh, what great discrimination!

garnisht: dressed (in fool's clothing).

for a tricksie . . . the matter: for the sake of wordplay go against sense.

how cherst thou: colloquial, as in 'How are you doing?'

Page 88
meane it, it: a mistake of some kind; Q2 amends to 'meane it, then'; some editors prefer Pope's emendation, 'merit it'.

paund: pawned, laid down to balance the stakes.

how so mere: howsoever.

disgest: digest. Lorenzo is punning, combining the natural (biological) meaning with the scholarly one of a digest as summary or condensation (as in *Reader's Digest*).

ile set you forth: I'll dish you up. Jessica is punning, adding to the domestic meaning (set out the food) the rhetorical notion of elaborate praise.

aunswere: answer to.

quallifie: moderate.

obdurate: too hard to change.

tiranny: unlimited power.

Page 89
thou but leadest . . . act: you are only carrying this demonstration of malice through to the last possible moment.

remorse: pity.

strange . . . strange: Now the Duke is playing with words, contrasting 'remarkable' with 'abnormal'. There is a hint of xenophobia here, confirmed ten lines later.

[129]

Endnotes

loose the forfaiture: cancel the penalty.

moytie: part.

this states: in error for *his state*. Q2 and F emend.

gentle: a particularly ironic instance of the pun on *Gentile*.

possest: informed.

Sabaoth: used here for 'sabbath', though in fact a different word, meaning 'armies', as in 'God of Sabaoth', Lord of Hosts.

baind: baned, poisoned.

Page 90
when the bagpipe . . . affection: when the bagpipe wheezes they cannot control their bladders.

for affection . . . or loathes: editors usually repunctuate and/or emend these lines; e.g. Mahood, following Bulloch, reads: '. . . urine: for affection/ Masters oft passion.' This would produce the following sense: 'for instinct often masters emotion, bending it in the direction of liking or loathing.'

in evitable: inevitable, unavoidable.

offend . . . offended: to embarrass himself (with wet breeches) because he cannot endure the bagpipe's noise.

lodgd: fixed.

certaine: unchanging.

currant: current, flow.

offence: injury.

question: debate; the term is interesting, however, in light of both the actual rapid exchange of questions just passed and the Quarto's excessive use of question marks.

bate: abate.

you may . . . Lambe: some copies of Q1 are defective here, and read
   well use question with the Woolfe,
   the Ewe bleake for the Lambe:

bleake: may be a dialect form of *bleat*.

fretten: fretted, tossed about.

that then which what's harder: in implied parenthesis ('and what could be harder than that?')

[130]

Endnotes

slavish parts: drudgery.

let their pallats . . . viands: let their palates be enlivened by the same food you eat.

deerely bought: cf. Portia's 'since you are deere bought', p. 82.

I stand for judgement: cf. Portia's 'I stand for sacrifice', p. 75.

determine: give a legal decision.

tainted: diseased.

weather: wether, a castrated ram.

meetest: the most appropriate.

soule . . . soule: not on the sole of your shoe but on your immortal soul.

inexecrable: most accursed.

and . . . accusd: it is a failure of justice that you still live.

Pythagoras: author of the theory of the transmigration of souls.

hangd: animals could be executed for their 'crimes' during the Middle Ages.

fell: deadly.

fleete: hasten away.

unhallowed dam: unholy mother.

raile: criticise violently.

controversie: printed as cotroversie in Q.

let his lacke . . . estimation: Do not allow his youth to be any obstacle to his getting a respectful recognition. With his quadrupled negatives, and the repetition of 'let . . . let', 'lacke . . . lacke', Bellario has made the grammatical disentangling of this sentence impossible, especially since 'let' means *both* 'permit' and 'hinder'; but the sense is visible none the less.

whose tryall . . . commendation: the test of whose abilities (in handling this trial) will do more for his reputation [than anything I can add].

difference . . . question: dispute which is here to be adjudicated.

enformed throughly: thoroughly briefed.

Endnotes

strange: an echo of the Duke's earlier criticism.

in such rule: so correct in procedure.

impugne: oppose.

within his danger: at his mercy.

confesse the bond: admit to the contract.

straind: constrained.

Page 94

to doe . . . little wrong: bend the law slightly, for a higher good.

Daniell: the incorruptible young judge who, in the Apocrypha, adjudicated between Susannah and the Elders.

Page 95

Not not for Venice: a mistake; F corrects to 'No, not for Venice.'

tenure: tenour, precise terms of the contract.

hath full relation . . . penaltie: fully applies to [even this] penalty.

ballance: scales.

on your charge: at your expense.

Page 96

still her use: her usual practice.

speake me faire: speak kindly of me (as in the proverbial, 'Speak well of the dead').

Barrabas: the condemned thief released by Pontius Pilate instead of Jesus; also the name of the protagonist in Marlowe's *Jew of Malta*.

Page 97

jote: jot, infinitesimally small amount.

Soft: steady, hold on.

a just pound: exactly a pound.

scruple: the scruple was an apothecary's measure, a little heavier than a gram (Mahood).

in the estimation of a hayre: by a hair's breadth.

Page 98

on the hip. Cf. Shylock's threat above, p. 47.

[132]

Endnotes

Ile . . . question: I won't wait around for any more discussion; but 'question' here is about to acquire the more sinister sense of 'criminal investigation'.

privie coffer: in England, the private resources of the monarch; therefore in some conflict with the idea of 'the generall state'.

Page 99
which humblenes . . . fine: which humility on your part may cause me to lower it to merely a fine.

I . . . not for Anthonio: Aye, that applies to the state's half, not to Anthonio's.

quit: remit.

in use: in trust; that is, Anthonio will have the use of the money during Shylock's life, and on his death it will be conveyed to Lorenzo and Jessica.

Shy. In christning . . . to the font: Q1 assigns this speech in error to Shylock instead of to Gratiano, who has been snapping at Shylock's heels for the last few minutes. Q2 emends. The point of the insult is that Shylock should have had a jury of twelve men to see him hanged rather than two godfathers to see him baptised.

Page 100
meete: proper.

gratifie: reward.

bound: obliged; but there is a subdued allusion to the almost fatal bond.

aquitted of: released from.

in lewe: in exchange.

cope: give in exchange for.

I pray you . . . againe: I ask you to recognise me/be intimate when next we meet. Portia reintroduces the sexual wordplay of the love plot.

Page 101
scuse: excuse.

in the morning: Bassanio plans to spend the night in Anthonio's house before returning home. Cf. p. 82 above.

ore-tane: overtaken.

[133]

Endnotes

Page 102

Troylus . . . Cressed: an allusion to the story of Troilus, the Trojan hero and son of Priam, and his ill-fated love for Cressida, who was traded to the Greeks and deserted him.

Thisbie: an allusion to the story of Pyramus and Thisbe, who were kept apart by their families, and an attempted night-time meeting resulted in their suicides.

Dido: the widowed queen of Carthage, Dido was abandoned by Aeneas, who had engaged in a temporary liaison with her during his flight from Troy and journey to become the founder of Rome.

Medea: Medea, a witch, helped Jason to carry off the Golden Fleece. Later she restored his father Aeson to youth; and later still she was abandoned by Jason.

steale from: escape from; but of course she literally stole from him also.

unthrift: cf. earlier uses of 'thrift' by Shylock.

Page 103

shrow: shrew.

nor we have not: nor have we; another double negative.

Post: messenger.

Stephen: in error for *Stephano*. Q2 emends.

Page 104

tutches: touches, strains.

pattens: either *patens*, the gold plates used in the Communion service, or in error for *patterns*.

quiring: choiring, singing.

muddy vesture of decay: mortal flesh.

unhandled colts: unbroken stallions.

make a mutuall stand: they all halt at the same moment.

the Poet: Ovid, in *Metamorphoses*, Book 10.

stockish: wooden.

nor is not moved: nor is moved; another double negative.

Terebus: in error for Erebus, the dark region between Earth and the Underworld.

Page 105

   naughty: worthless.

   without respect: except in relation to other things.

   attended: accompanied (by the other).

   Renne: wren.

   How many . . . perfection: the play on *season . . . seasond* (timing, spiced up) cannot survive paraphrase; roughly, how many things are only fully appreciated and perfected by perfect timing.

   Endimion: Phoebe (Diana), the moon-goddess, fell in love with the shepherd Endymion, whom she entranced so that he would never wake and leave her.

   which speed . . . our words: whom we hope have been all the more successful thanks to our words.

Page 106

   We should . . . the sunne: we should have the same hours of daylight as they do in the Antipodes (Australia) if you are going to be walking about in the dark; i.e. you will turn the cycle of day and night upside down.

   be light: be frivolous, unreliable.

   God sort all: God disposes.

   in all sence: perhaps 'in all senses', since Portia here uses 'bound' in at least three: indebted; imprisoned; and contracted (in bond to Shylock).

   acquitted of: released from.

   scant: cut short.

   breathing curtesie: verbal politeness.

   gelt: gelded, castrated.

   posie: motto.

   Cutlers poetry: knife-maker's verses.

   You swore to me when I did give you: the line is unmetrical. Q2 emends: 'You swore to me when I did give *it* you.'

   respective: circumspect.

Page 107

   the Clarke . . . had it: the clerk who got it will never grow a beard.

Endnotes

slightly: easily.

Page 108
containe: retain.

wanted . . . ceremonie: would have been so brash as to insist on having something of such symbolic value.

civill Doctor: a qualified civil lawyer.

beset . . . besmere it: attacked by shame and the demands of courtesy; my honour refused to be so stained by ingratitude.

candels: stars.

liberall: free and easy.

Page 109
Know him: sleep with him; cf. Portia's previous *double-entendre*, p. 100.

Argos: the watchman Argus, employed by the Greek gods, especially to guard their wives, because he had a hundred eyes.

take him . . . pen: then let me not catch him in the act, for if I do, I'll blunt his pen/penis.

enforced wrong: this wrong I was forced to do you.

an oath of credite: ironic; a promise one can trust!

miscaried: been ruined.

advisedly: knowingly.

Why this is like . . . faire enough: this is like mending the roads in summer when there are no potholes; i.e. digging up dirt unnecessarily.

Page 110
You shall not know: has Portia invented the letter as a ruse for rebuilding Anthonio's capital out of her own resources?

lyving: the means whereby to make a living.

Page 111
intergotories: sworn examinations of witness or defendant; the last item of legal vocabulary.

ring: orifice; the last sexual *double-entendre*.

Appendix

The comicall Hiſtory of the Merchant of Venice.

Enter *Anthonio, Salaryno,* and *Salanio.*

An. IN ſooth I know not why I am ſo ſad,
It wearies me, you ſay it wearies you;
But how I caught it, found it, or came by it,
What ſtuffe tis made of, whereof it is borne,
I am to learne : and ſuch a want-wit ſadnes
makes of mee,
That I haue much adoe to know my ſelfe.

Salarino. Your minde is toſſing on the Ocean,
There where your Argoſies with portlie ſayle
Like Signiors and rich Burgars on the flood,
Or as it were the Pageants of the ſea,
Doe ouer-peere the petty traffiquers
That curſie to them do them reuerence
As they flie by them with theyr wouen wings.

Salanio. Beleeue mee ſir, had I ſuch venture forth,
The better part of my affections would
Be with my hopes abroade. I ſhould be ſtill
Plucking the graſſe to know where ſits the wind,
Piring in Maps for ports, and peers and rodes :
And euery obiect that might make me feare
Miſ-fortune to my ventures, out of doubt
Would make me ſad.

Salar. My wind cooling my broth,
vvould blow me to an ague when I thought
vvhat harme a winde too great might doe at ſea.
I ſhould not ſee the ſandie howre-glaſſe runne
But I ſhould thinke of ſhallowes and of flatts,
And ſee my wealthy *Andrew* docks in ſand

A 2.   Vayling

Vayling her high top lower then her ribs
To kisse her buriall; should I goe to Church
And see the holy edifice of stone
And not bethinke me straight of dangerous rocks,
vvhich touching but my gentle vessels side
vvould scatter all her spices on the streame,
Enrobe the roring waters with my silkes,
And in a word, but euen now worth this,
And now worth nothing. Shall I haue the thought
To thinke on this, and shall I lack the thought
That such a thing bechaunc'd would make me sad?
But tell not me, I know *Anthonio*
Is sad to thinke vpon his merchandize.

  Anth. Beleeue me no, I thanke my fortune for it
My ventures are not in one bottome trusted,
Nor to one place; nor is my whole estate
Vpon the fortune of this present yeere:
Therefore my merchandize makes me not sad.

  Sola. Why then you are in loue.

  Anth. Fie, fie.

  Sola. Not in loue neither: then let vs say you are sad
Becaufe you are not merry; and twere as easie
For you to laugh and leape, and say you are merry
Becaufe you are not sad. Now by two-headed *Ianus*,
Nature hath framd strange fellowes in her time:
Some that will euermore peepe through their eyes,
And laugh like Parrats at a bagpyper.
And other of such vinigar aspect,
That theyle not shew theyr teeth in way of smile
Though *Nestor* sweare the iest be laughable.

              Enter *Bassanio, Lorenso,* and *Gratiano.*

  Sola. Here comes *Bassanio* your most noble kinsman,
Gratiano, and *Lorenso.* Faryewell,
We leaue you now with better company.

  Sala. I would haue staid till I had made you merry,
If worthier friends had not preuented me.

  Anth. Yout worth is very deere in my regard.

1

I take it your owne busines calls on you,
And you embrace th'occasion to depart.

  Sal. Good morrow my good Lords.

  Bass. Good signiors both when shal we laugh : say, when ?
You grow exceeding strange : must it be so ?

  Sal. Weele make our leysures to attend on yours.

                                    Exeunt Salarino, and Solanio.

  Lor. My Lord *Bassanio,*since you haue found *Anthonio*
We two will leaue you, but at dinner time
I pray you haue in minde where we must meete.

  Bass. I will not faile you.

  Grat. You looke not well signior *Anthonio,*
You haue too much respect vpon the world :
They loose it that doe buy it with much care,
Beleeue me you are meruailously changd.

  Ant. I hold the world but as the world *Gratiano,*
A stage, where euery man must play a part,
And mine a sad one.

  Grati. Let me play the foole,
With mirth and laughter let old wrinckles come,
And let my liuer rather heate with wine
Then my hart coole with mortifying grones.
Why should a man whose blood is warme within,
Sit like his grandsire, cut in Alablaster ?
Sleepe when he wakes ? and creepe into the Iaundies
By beeing peeuish ? I tell thee what *Anthonio,*
I loue thee, and tis my loue that speakes :
There are a sort of men whose visages
Doe creame and mantle like a standing pond,
And doe a wilful stilnes entertaine,
With purpose to be drest in an opinion
Of wisedome grauitie, profound conceit,
As who should say, I am sir Oracle,
And when I ope my lips, let no dogge barke.
O my *Anthonio* I doe know of these
That therefore onely are reputed wise

                                    A 3.   For